How-to Advanced Custom
Motorcycle Chassis

Doug Mitchel

Published by:
Wolfgang Publications Inc.
Stillwater, MN 55082
www.wolfpub.com

Legals

First published in 2007 by Wolfgang Publications Inc.,
Stillwater MN 55082

The information in this book is true and complete to the best of our
knowledge. All recommendations are made without any guarantee
on the part of the author or publisher, who also disclaim any liability
incurred in connection with the use of this data or specific details.

We recognize that some words, model names and designations, for
example, mentioned herein are the property of the trademark holder.
We use them for identification purposes only. This is not an official
publication.

ISBN number: 1-929133-37-5
Printed and bound in China

How-to Advanced Custom Motorcycle Chassis

Acknowledgements

As it goes with any of the book projects I become involved in, it is only with the help of many friends and associates that the final product becomes possible. Although a bit different in scope than my other titles, this effort required the never ending patience and assistance from the following people:

- Bryan Davies at Arlen Ness Motorcycles

- Anthony Underwood at Baker Drivetrain

- Jason and Bethany at Chopsmiths

- John Parham and Jeff Carstensen of J&P Cycles

- John Dodson from Johnny Legend Customs

- Johnny Lange, Strip Club Choppers

- Ron Starrantino at Von Dutch Kustom Motorcycles

-John Lewis at Xtreme Cycle Tech

DEDICATION:

To Nancy G for helping a long lost friend.

Introduction

There comes a day in many men's and women's lives when the urge to create something takes over their common sense. In the case when two wheels are involved, we hope to provide some guidance with this book.

There are many paths that can be taken when you embark on the building of a custom motorcycle, and we certainly haven't covered them all here. We have exposed you to a variety of ideas that should help you mold your own machine. Some may feel the need to turn to the experts for some of the related assemblies and processes, which is certainly an option as well. By illustrating what's required in the simplest form, we can show you the proper method of getting the job done right the first time. Some of the current programs on TV make building a custom motorcycle look easy, but they tend to gloss over some of the more intricate procedures. Leaving them out of the build would find you with a machine that was 73% complete. Using a big orange hammer to bang things into place may look like fun, but as the real experts will tell you there should never be any hammering to make things fit. Makes for exciting TV maybe, but it's hardly a real world truth.

It is not whether you build it yourself or have someone do it for you, but that you ride with pride that matters most. Figure out what you want to create, check the catalogs, and with the experts, and get started. It's never too late, and always a great journey once you've taken those first steps.

Have fun and ride safe!

Chapter One

The Chassis

The Foundation for Everything Else

Odds are, if you are reading this book you have already seen the TV shows, and read the books and related periodicals. You're ready to build your own motorcycle from the ground up, or add some serious modifications to your existing ride. With the growing interest in this field you are certainly not alone, and we hope this book will assist you as you wade into the project.

Regardless of what style motorcycle you plan to build, the entire machine will be assembled around the chassis. Once this fact has been acknowledged, you'll need to decide what path to

Built on a Redneck frame, this long roadster was built twice. The second assembly is the work of Bob's Shop in Milwaukee. Engine is a 127 Ultima mated to a Baker 6-speed tranny. The long and low look is the result of a frame with 5 inches of stretch and a 46 degree neck. Mean Streets fork sits in 3 degree trees. Jeff Zwieg

follow. The market is filled with terrific offerings in ready to build units, or you may take the more drastic step of creating one from scratch. While daunting, that route is not impossible as long as certain rules are followed.

Frames come in a variety of styles with a host of different features. The chassis you select must have the dimensions and features that fit the design criteria for your new motorcycle. To say that the frame has a major impact on how the bike looks and handles is a serious understatement. A radically stretched frame with 38 degrees of rake will look and handle much differently than a more traditional non-stretched frame with a 30 degree fork angle. Your choice of frame will affect many of the other choices you make later in the project. Careful planning before you put the first wrench into action is crucial to positive and manageable results. Trying to change one style of frame into something else is a recipe for disaster, so make your plans first, then buy.

THE DESIGN

It all boils down to the way you intend to use the bike. If you're building a short-haul, "bar hopping" bike, then comfort or carrying capacity doesn't rate high on the list of considerations. Looking cool is great, but frame geometry and the ability to turn corners are key factors when actually taking your new mount to the streets. The least expensive frames are OEM-style chassis that accept fenders and gas tanks with stock dimensions,

DD Custom Cycle chose a War Eagle Conqueror chassis for this creation. The tear-drop down tube is an unusual feature that melded neatly with the rest of the execution. A 250 series rear tire is fitted with left side drive, and every inch of sheet metal is of DD Custom Cycle's design.

Taking the path of most resistance, Chopsmiths built the Speed Goblin using an all steel frame of their own design and construction. The sturdy concept includes a single-sided swingarm and is reminiscent of the early board track racing machines.

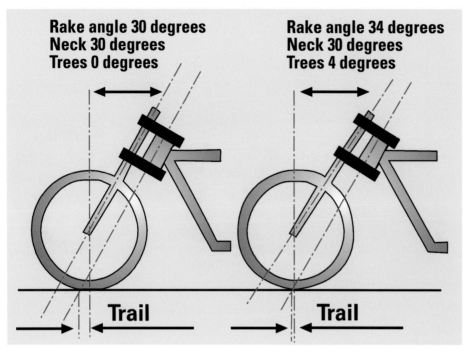

Rake angle 30 degrees
Neck 30 degrees
Trees 0 degrees

Rake angle 34 degrees
Neck 30 degrees
Trees 4 degrees

In the case of a stock frame where the rider is looking to add some rake without cutting the frame, a set of raked trees can eliminate most of the positive trail and make for an unstable, unsafe motorcycle. Use one of the charts mentioned in the text to figure the rake and trail before ordering raked trees.

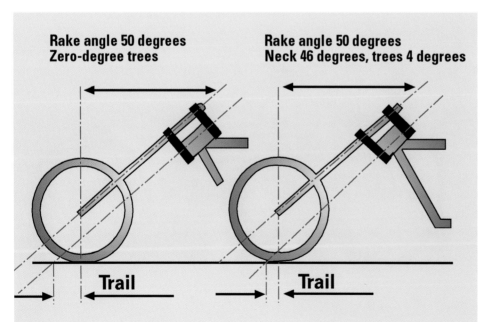

Rake angle 50 degrees
Zero-degree trees

Rake angle 50 degrees
Neck 46 degrees, trees 4 degrees

This is a better use of raked trees - many experienced chopper builders get part of their total rake from the trees. In this way they reduce the excess trail that generally comes with rake angles of 40 degrees or more. By reducing the trail they eliminate the heavyness and "flop" that often comes with extreme rake angles. Trail calculators can be found at perseperformance.com or Google "trail calculator."

which doesn't make a lot of difference because few builders assemble a "stock" Milwaukee-style bike. If you desired a bike that looked like your neighbors, you wouldn't be scheming to build a full-bore custom. The other relatively inexpensive design is the chopper frame, though some of these aren't exactly what you would call cheap. As always, you have to pay for the extra sex appeal that comes with the wide rear-section and the brand name. One other major consideration in using a "factory" frame is that all the math has been done, as well as the welding and pre-assembly. A nicely printed instruction manual is a handy thing as well, and creating a bike from scratch won't afford you that luxury.

Assuming you've chosen the pre-assembled chassis route, take some time to check with builders and local shops to see if any brands stand out as being easier or more difficult to use as your platform. Some shops may balk when asked too many questions, since you are basically taking work off their plates when building your own, but others will consider the fact that you may encounter some trouble later that will require a professional's touch, and you'll keep them in mind.

TERMS

Before delving further into a discussion of frames, let's get a grip on some remedial terms.

Rake:

Rake is the angle of the neck (and often the fork assembly) when compared to vertical. Some builders talk about a frame being "raked five degrees." What they mean is that it has five additional degrees of rake as compared to stock.

Trail:

Trail is the distance between the front tire's contact patch and the point where the centerline of the bike's steering axis meets the ground (see the illustrations). Motorcycles have positive trail, the contact patch is behind the point where the centerline meets the road. Much like the caster angle of an automobile, positive trail provides the straight line stability that allows us to take our hands off the bars while going down the road.

Many people think rake and trail are essentially the same, but this assumption will quickly lead to a major conflict. However, with most standard-issue front fork assemblies and standard triple trees an increase in rake will result in an increase in positive trail. These dimensions can be created or altered through several factors. The angle of the steering head is one, while the angle of the chosen triple-trees is another.

Where you can get into trouble is with aftermarket triple trees that provide additional rake, installed without changing the angle of the frame's neck. If you spend a little time with a pencil and paper doing sketches, you will

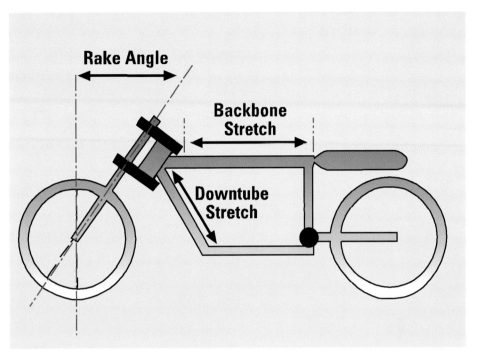

There are actually two kinds of "stretch", as shown here. Often a frame will be described as being "4 inches out and 2 up", meaning 4 inches of backbone stretch and 2 inches of down tube stretch.

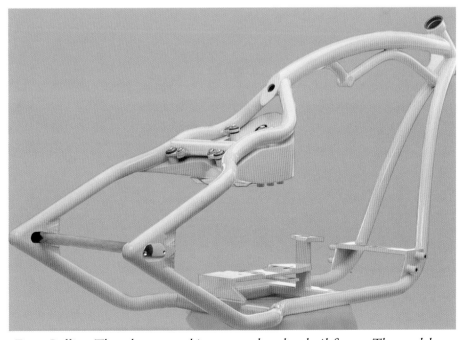

From Rolling Thunder comes this very modern hardtail frame. The model shown is designed to accept an Evo drivetrain, though you can order it ready to accept a Twin Cam B. Most frame manufacturers have a long list of possible options.

Precious Metal Customs will be happy to build you a complete custom cycle to meet your needs or simply provide you with a frame to build your own. This version utilizes a swingarm in the rear, but rigid models can also be had. Precious Metal Customs

The latest creation from Arlen Ness Motorcycles is "Nessed Up" and shows us one way an owner can tweak a touring mount for the custom world. Arlen Ness Motorcycles

see that "raked trees" decrease rake. Understand further that the blanket statement, "it's always bad to decrease trail" can't be made. As always it depends on the individual bike and frame.

In a situation where you are adding rake to a stock frame with a set of five degree trees, you run the risk of adding rake and decreasing the trail to nearly zero. Chopper frames, on the other hand, with extreme rake angles of 40 and 50 degrees can often end up with too much positive trail and that really heavy feeling when turning at slow speeds. Many experienced chopper builders will buy a frame with 40 degrees of rake and then use a set of five-degree trees for a total of 45 degrees of rake. By using the five-degree trees they reduce the trail to a more manageable level and get rid of that really heavy feeling.

Stretch:

The current popularity of choppers and bikes with raised necks means that we have two types of "stretch." More typical stretch refers to material added to the top tube – sometimes called the backbone. Thus a frame that is "stretched two inches" is two inches longer between the seat and the steering neck than it was originally (or than a similar factory frame). To raise the neck, manufacturers often add material or stretch the frame's downtubes. Thus if you ask a frame builder about the dimensions of a new frame they might say it's, "three inches ahead and two inches up," meaning the neck is positioned three inches ahead and two inches higher than a "stock" frame. All of these options will affect the ride and handling of your machine, so be sure to think about the frame's specifications before you sign the order form. And if the specs you want are out of the ordinary, ask for some advice from an experienced builder.

FRAME STYLES
Hardtail or soft-tail

In the old days frames were mostly of the hard-tail variety, with soft-tail or twin-shock designs following later. Today we have those same choices, joined by new varieties of the same. As with any aspect of the custom world, a builder's imagination is about the only limit.

HARDTAIL

As the name implies, a hardtail (also called a rigid) frame incorporates no rear suspension in its design. These frames are simpler to manufacture and thus may offer a less expensive entry for anyone starting on a scratch-built project. The lack of suspension means a hardtail frame can be the foundation for a strictly-business kind of hot rod machine. Hardtail frames have great lines and the look of a classic V-twin motorcycle, but the down side is the fact that the lack of rear suspension compromises comfort.

Nothing really says "Chopper" like a hardtail with an extra long fork, and the decision to build a true hardtail will depend solely on your riding agenda and tolerance for discomfort.

This rolling chassis kit from American Thunder comes with rear fender and gas tank, and mounts for both, which makes assembly by a non-professional much, much easier.

The frame determines the silhouette of the bike. In this case that silhouette will be long and low, note the somewhat extreme rake angle and the dropped neck. Rolling Thunder

Here you can see how the shocks (air-ride shocks in this case) mount on a typical soft-tail suspension - under the transmission mounting plate. Unlike a twin-shock design, these shocks get longer as the bike goes over a bump.

SOFT-TAIL STYLE

By hiding the shocks under the frame a soft-tail style chassis provides the look of a hardtail without the harsh ride. Soft-tail style framcs can be the basis for some very good looking custom bikes, with lines and simplicity unmatched by twin-shock frames. Some riders think a soft-tail frame is the only one to have, and the only way to build a bike with the right look. As with every decision that needs to be made, there are very few wrong answers, and a myriad of ways to achieve your goal.

For all the styling advantages of a soft-tail style frame there is however, a penalty. Essentially the soft-tail style design allows for limited suspension travel, meaning the ride will never match that of most twin-shock bikes. When you lower the bike you end up with even less travel.

NOT QUITE A SOFT-TAIL

If the goal is to hide the shocks and create a pseudo-hardtail, then there's no reason the shocks have to be under the transmission. Or, even if they are, that they have to follow exactly the configuration laid out by Milwaukee. There are a few frames that hide the shocks without following the standard soft-tail configuration, and another group that uses the under-transmission shock location to support a tubular swingarm that doesn't even try to look like an extension of the frame.

Dan Roche's bike started life as a Daytec soft-tail frame with 7 inches of stretch and a 2 inch dropped neck. Dan added the outboard shocks to make it a better drag-race chassis (one of Dan's hobbies). Power comes from a 139 inch Kendall Johnson/S&S motor. Wheels measure 18 inches, rear tire is a 300.

TWIN-SHOCK

Twin-shock frames have been manufactured for a long time. This is a tried and true design providing plenty of suspension travel and generally good handling and ride. Twin-shock frames make it easy to adjust the ride height in the rear by installing longer or shorter shock absorbers. Even adjusting their mounting position can achieve a different ride, but this modification has its limitations. Though most soft-tail style frames mount the motor to the frame in a solid fashion, many twin-shock frames feature "rubber-mounted" engines. By suspending the engine and transmission in rubber the vibes of an Evo or non "B" TC engine, are isolated from the rider for a smoother ride and minimized fatigue after a long day in the saddle. The disadvantages of the twin-shock design include the look, which you may or may not like.

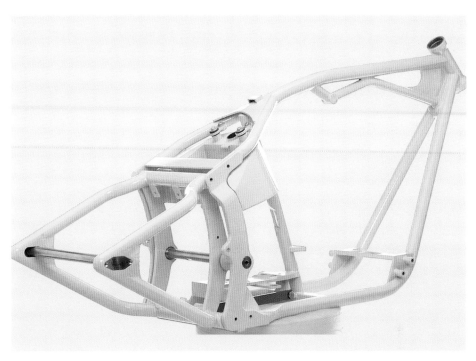

This soft-tail frame holds true to the original design, with a swingarm that provides the look and lines of a hardtail. This particular example will accept a 300 tire and can be ordered in a variety of different rake and stretch dimensions. Rolling Thunder

POWER, POWER, POWER

Along with the style of frame you also have to consider which type of engine you want to use to get this new beast down the road (note the engine section in Chapter Two). Options include the tried and true Evo-style engine from Milwaukee or the aftermarket, and the newer Twin Cam from Harley-Davidson (and the aftermarket as well), available with or without the counter-balancers (the B version).

Many hardtail and soft-tail style chassis bolt the engine

The aftermarket makes such a wide variety of parts that it's easy to build a Right Side Drive Panhead. Something you hardly ever saw in 1969.

Q&A: Michael from Revolution

Michael Kamalian, owner of Revolution, is the man who figured out how to make frames and wheels from carbon fiber. A true innovator, Michael has a very interesting story to tell.

Michael, give us some background and tell us how you came to manufacture frames and wheels from carbon fiber?

I'm a physician by trade, my specialty is chiropractic sports medicine. In 1994 I bought a Harley, then I wanted to customize the bike. About a year later I was getting ready to graduate and a friend said we should buy a local motorcycle shop, just for something to do until we became licensed. I thought why not? I could run the shop and then tear it down later and put up a clinic.

However, the shop was making good money so we stayed in the business. At about the same time I met Greg Collins, who's been customizing bikes for years and years. Greg has been a great deal of help to me. Eventually we did sell the motorcycle business and I worked overseas for about a year.

I started Revolution in 2003. At about the same time I got into prototype car racing, 24 hours of Daytona, Sebring, things like that. So I knew about carbon fiber, how light and strong it is. During a plane ride I did some sketches of a motorcycle frame made entirely of carbon fiber. Some of my friends who worked at Hot Bike said, "it can't be done." So it became a bet. Two years later we unveiled the prototype. Then last year we introduced the wheels.

Our frame weighs 40 lbs, while a standard bobber frame is probably 100 lbs. Our wheels are likewise very light and very strong. We are at the point now where guys who are leaders in the industry are starting to buy the wheels. People

Q&A: Michael from Revolution

like Russell from Exile, Skeeter Todd from Rolling Thunder and Brian Klock from Klock Werks are buying my parts for their bikes and their build-off bikes.

Why do I want two of your wheels?

These are for performance guys who want the most for the money. You spend eleven thousand dollars on the engine and all the rest to have a fast and powerful motorcycle. Then you spend three thousand dollars on two 40 lb rotating blocks of aluminum at either end of the bike. Our largest wheel - 8.5X18 inches - weights nine pounds with hub and bearings. A similar wheel in aluminum weighs forty pounds.

To expand a little on the weight savings: The outer rim affects 85% of the overall performance of the wheel, the spokes affect 10% of the performance of the wheel, and the hub affects 5% of the performance of the wheel – we've made them all lighter. We have reduced the weight where it increases performance most, something we can uniquely achieve due to the fact that we can manipulate the material. If we reduce the weight in the correct places we save on rotational inertia and physics takes care of the rest. Reduced rotational mass is easier to spin and as such, the motor has more usable power output as it wastes less to spin the wheel. The same thing works in reverse for braking. It's the rotation of the wheel that the brakes stop, not just the weight of the bike. The lighter the wheels, the less rotational inertia and the easier the bike is to stop.

I just put a set of our wheels on an old digger project bike that had billet wheels. When I put the bike on the dyno with our new carbon fiber wheels we got 17 additional horsepower at the rear wheel. I would not have believed it if I hadn't seen it. The average we see is a 10 to 15 percent horsepower increase.

What is the down-side to these wheels?

Other than cost, there really isn't a downside. They are 10 times stronger than Aluminum. We dropped one off a four-story parking ramp and it just bounced, you can't do that to Aluminum. They can't bend. The amount of force that it takes to fracture one is over 10gs. And they won't rust, corrode or fatigue. They're cool and you can paint them just like fiberglass. Right now Boeing Aircraft and the US military have driven up the cost. Pretty soon though the supply and demand curves will come into balance and then the price will come down.

Explain the material and how it's manufactured for those of us who aren't familiar with carbon fiber?

Once the material is woven into carbon cloth it is infused with resin. The impregnated carbon fiber must then be kept at 50 degrees or less so it won't "kick." For that reason the material is shipped refrigerated. You can work with it as long as it's kept cold.

We use 280 gram, pre-impregnated carbon fiber. That material is hand laid into steel molds, vacuum bagged and placed in an autoclave. The wheel molds are two-piece so they can be pulled apart to release the wheel. We use a silicone plug inside each spoke so they hold a real nice shape. The autoclave looks like a mini submarine, most wheels are cooked at 150 psi and 300 degrees. The pressure helps the shape and the high temperature makes the chemical reaction occur.

Once they pop from the autoclave the wheel is trued and the lip is machined to a tolerance of .001 inch. They are truly perfect. Then the hubs are pressed in with 100 tons of force, you would have to destroy the wheel to get them apart. People don't always understand that carbon gets its strength in the shape, our tubes are extremely strong.

S&S produces a variety of V-twin motors, the 96 inch, in natural finish, is one of the most basic ways to power your custom build. Biker's Choice/S&S

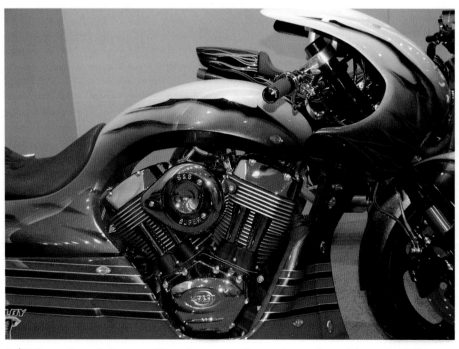

S&S has released the new X-wedge motor for use in real-world custom bikes. The engine uses a 56 degree V, and three belt-driven camshafts: one for both intake valves, and one for each exhaust valve.

solid to the frame. If the engine is a TC 88B with counter-balancers, then that isn't a problem. If however, the engine is a 113 cubic inch aftermarket mill from TP Engineering, then you have to understand that the engine will shake, and all those vibes will be transmitted directly to your body. New motor options also include those that look vintage, but are assembled using modern day technology. By combining the look of a Pan or Shovelhead motor with contemporary reliability, you get the best of both worlds. This option will allow you to build a machine that looks every inch retro while providing up to date technology and dependability.

HOW TO CHOOSE THE RIGHT ONE

The frame decision will affect, and be effected by, your choice of an engine and your feelings about style and your riding needs. First you need to decide where you want the shocks, or if there should be any shocks at all. Though most builders want more radical designs, there are some near-copies of factory soft-tail and FXR frames on the market. Not only are these frames often less expensive to buy, they are generally less expensive to equip as well. These chassis will accept stock hardware and sheet metal, which tends to be the least expensive to buy new, or can be found by trolling a swap meet or maybe hangin' from a nail in your buddy's garage. Though a few years ago everyone had to have at least a 250 tire, today a lot of people are happy with a 180 or 200 tire on the back.

When searching for a frame, remember that some of the non-OEM or "custom" frames are fairly raw and have no tabs for mounting sheet metal or gas tanks. This translates into more work and expense. Many frame manufacturers offer a build sheet, much like the option list available when you buy a new car. With this sheet you can specify dimensions and the type of sheet metal you plan to use before getting a frame that will challenge your abilities.

BUY QUALITY

When it comes to buying a frame there are a number of important points to consider. Arlen Ness explaines that you need a frame that's straight, but there's more to it than that.

"You need to be sure everything is straight and true. All the parts should bolt to the frame without having to take a file to the holes. Look for high quality welds. Some shops don't do a very good job of fitting the tubes together. Where one tube fits to another they don't do a nice concave cutout. The fit is poor so they just fill the gap up with weld material."

"If you buy a cheap frame and the welds are rough, and you have to mold the welds, you might

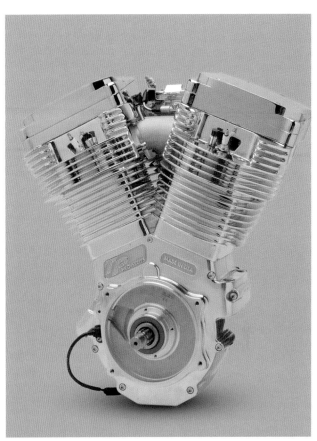

Based on a 4-1/8th inch bore and 4-5/8 inch stroke, this rowdy 124 comes from TP with 10.2:1 compression, .630/.650 cam, roller rockers and 1.65/2.00 inch valves to achieve 124 horses and 130 ft. lbs.

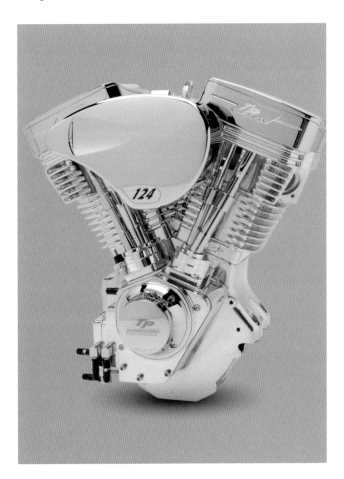

If there's a Ferrari of V-Twin motor it has to be TP Engineering - the company that makes billet sculpture masquerading as kick ass engines. TP

end up spending more money than if you bought the more expensive frame in the first place. We try to have frames with really nice welds so you don't have to do any molding." With all his years in the business, it pays to listen to Arlen.

FINAL THOUGHTS

Before spending money on any frame ask yourself the following questions: How and where will the bike be ridden? What style of bike are you planning on building? Will this be a simple machine that retains the stock dimensions and basic sheet metal, or a more unusual bike that requires more exotic sheet metal? Do you need or want an ultra fat rear wheel? How powerful should the motorcycle be? How much of the work will you do yourself? What is your budget for the complete project?

When it comes to deciding whether or not you need the wide tire, huge motor, or the billet wheels and stretched frame, it comes down to money. If money were no object most of us would build a really killer machine. Living in the real world however, dictates that each project cost no more than our budget allows.

There are plenty of frames out there in the shops and catalogs. Everything from short Bobber frames designed for Sportster/Buell drivetrains, to extra long chopper frames with 45 and 50 degrees of rake. No matter which one you buy, be sure you get a high quality frame with the dimensions and features that fit and match the rest of your project. Take your time, do the homework and be sure to start with a chassis that meets all of your needs and cost considerations.

TITLE CONSIDERATIONS

When you build a motorcycle from scratch based on a Chopper Guys frame, it will be titled as a Chopper Guys, not as a Harley-Davidson. Many states will title a scratch-built bike as a reconstructed vehicle, the same as a car or motorcycle that's been rebuilt from a wreck. What follows are general guidelines for the process of obtaining a title. Many states require you to bring the bike to the state Motor Vehicle Testing Station for an inspection. A few states make it very difficult to register a scratch-built bike. Each state is a little different (your mileage may vary) so take a minute before you start on the project and call the state to inquire exactly what they require, this is covered again in Chapter 2.

When you buy a frame, engine cases, or a complete engine from any legitimate aftermarket supplier you will get a MSO (Manufacturers Statement of Origin). Be sure it is filled out correctly and that any previous transfers are noted. If the paper work isn't clean don't buy the parts. Before providing a title for a scratch-built bike most states

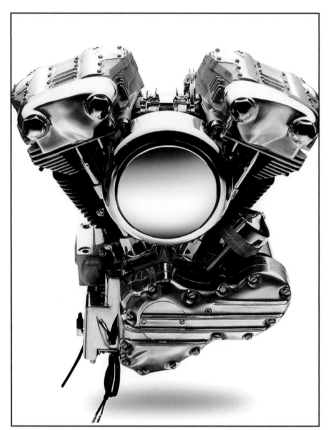

"Knucklehead" Evos are available for those who want the look without the maintenance - complete with "generator" style cam covers. Jammer

Avoid the high cost of upgrading a factory Twin Cam. Just belly up to the bar and order a compete 124 cubic inch Twin Cam from S&S. Bolts up to stock frames and transmissions.

require that you provide them with the MSO with serial numbers noted for both the engine cases and the frame.

A complete used engine might not be such a hot deal, unless you buy it from a reputable dealer who can provide the necessary paperwork. It's also not a good idea to base your new engine on a set of used Harley-Davidson cases. Without an MSO the state will probably not give you a title for the new bike.

You must keep the receipts for everything you buy. The idea is to prove to the state that the parts are not stolen and also that the sales tax has already been paid on all the parts. Sometimes people buy a set of new aftermarket engine cases and then a complete engine, minus cases, from a private party or at a swap meet. Then they install the used internals into the new, legal cases. The result is a cheap, legal engine. Life is good until it comes time to prove to the state that you bought everything, including the pistons, flywheel assembly, cylinders, and so on.

Use a bit of common sense when buying used parts. Get receipts when you can, especially for big-ticket items. If the price of a used part seems too good to be true, ask yourself why. It doesn't make sense to buy parts from questionable sources, you're only supporting the people who might steal your motorcycle next.

Shops that build bikes professionally recommend that you keep perfect records and paperwork during the project. Most keep a duplicate file as the state has been known to lose a complete file. Creating a photo record, to back up the paperwork, is a good idea too. It all sounds like a lot of extra labor, but the end result will be a custom motorcycle that can be titled without too much grief from the state you live in.

Another example of the new X-wedge in a real world custom, built in this case by the Arlen Ness shop. Eventually available in 110 to 139 cubic inch displacements, the Wedge is S&S' answer to future EPA and noise requirements.

The range of available frames is truly amazing. At the Rolling Thunder booth they have everything from Twin Cam Bagger frames to Evo hardtail chassis set up for the skinny, or fat, rear tire of your choice.

Chapter Two

Frames & Swingarms

Various Styles & Dimensions

Chapter One took a brief look at the frame, and the role the frame plays in the creation of your custom scoot. The purpose of this chapter is to delve more deeply into the design and configurations offered, allowing you to make a more educated decision. What makes a good frame, what

materials go into a quality frame and who makes the frames for sale on the market today?

We've also created a section on swingarms. In many cases you can add the fat tire of your dreams to your current ride without replacing the entire frame – just the swingarm. Also new is a section

From the guys best known for unique hardtail frames comes this very slick and equally unique mono-shock, no-downtube frame designed for a Buell/Sportster drivetrain. Build the ultimate hooligan bike with the rake of your choice and a drivetrain borrowed from some inexpensive donor bike. Kool doesn't have to be expensive. Redneck

on engines, which one to pick and what are the trade offs. The frame market is changing so fast we've decided to offer information on trends in the market and some of the features available from the various frame manufacturers. Be sure to check out the frame fabrication chapter at the back of the book for a look at the techniques that go into the manufacture of a quality frame.

Both the frame and swingarm section attempt to provide as much information as possible to individuals who want to run one of the wider 250, 300 or 330 series tires. With that in mind we've included a number of the new right side drive Big-Twin frames and the Baker transmission that makes the right side drive a viable option for the mega-rubber designs.

As you ride down the road the action of braking and burnouts puts enormous stress on the frame. If the frame is well constructed those stresses will result in little or no frame flex. The basic idea is to build a simple, strong structure. It's especially important that the neck and swingarm areas be strong enough to effectively resist the loads that are concentrated in those two areas.

MATERIALS

Most of the aftermarket frames are constructed from mild steel, a few use chrome-moly tubing. As the owner of one fabrication shop explained, "for most of these frames, no one did a computerized engineering study. They didn't do a

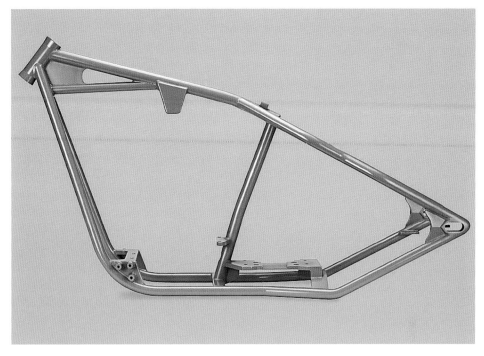

Catering to the varying desires of today's custom crowd, Daytec sells this 4 inch stretch frame that carries a 250 series tire and wheel in its rigid tubes. Biker's Choice/Daytec

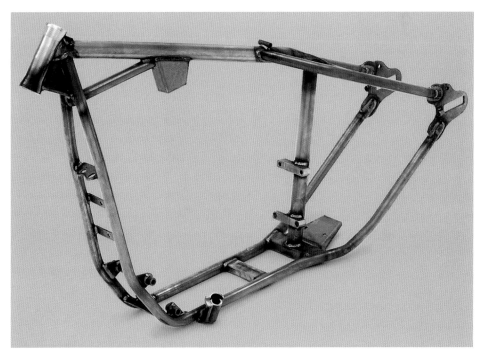

Paughco also does its best to meet the needs of every builder and provides this rigid Sportster frame for use with 1986 through 2001 running gear. Biker's Choice/Paughco

Mild steel and moly come with various wall dimensions. Thicker wall tubing is sometimes used not only because it's stronger but to absorb vibration. C. Maida

At Rolling Thunder they keep a large stock of mostly mild steel, DOM tubing in stock. C. Maida

material analysis of mild steel, they chose it because experience taught them that mild steel tubing, of a certain quality in a certain size and wall thickness, was plenty strong enough."

Though chrome-moly might be the stronger material you can't simply say that chrome-moly frames are better than those built from mild steel. It is often the execution of the design as well as the geometry involved that will make one type of steel a better choice than another.

TOUGH MOLY - MILD STEEL

You can't talk about motorcycle frames and frame design without talking about what they are made from. As we said most frames are welded together from mild steel, a few are built all, or in part, from chrome-moly.

Before trying to decide which material is better suited to the manufacture of motorcycle frames it might be best if we first answered the question: What is mild steel? And for help in this department we have the input of Jim Petrykowski, owner of the Metal Fab shop in Blaine, Minnesota.

"What we call mild steel is available in a wide variety of shapes and forms. The lowest grade of steel is E.R. Buttweld. This stuff looks like exhaust tubing, and the grain is random because it is essentially cold rolled sheet steel cut into strips, rolled up and welded (the E.R. stands for electric-resistance, as in arc welding). It's inexpensive and widely produced."

"This tubing is moderately strong, but the seam is a problem. If you form or bend it, it will break at the weld, and it's not uniform in size. What's called DOM (drawn over mandrel) is made by taking larger diameter tubing with a welded seam, and drawing it over a die set. Usually you're 'necking down' the tubing to a somewhat smaller size by drawing it through the die with a bullet-shaped tool in the center."

"By drawing the tubing through the tooling the size becomes more uniform, the wall thickness increases and the strength of the material increases. The weakness of the weld is minimized and the tubing can now be more easily formed and bent. Basically the steel companies take rather weak raw tubing and make it much stronger. Top of the line tubing is seamless. The easiest way to form seamless tubing is by taking red hot solid bar stock, piercing it and then pulling it through a mandrel."

"The very highest quality tubing is cold-drawn seamless, in which case a billet of bar stock is pierced and drawn through dies while it's cold, with lubrication. This process gets the material's grain going in one direction which makes it easier to bend and form."

"To form steel you take iron, add manganese and carbon and re-fire it. Once it's molten you draw off the impurities and what's left is steel. The more carbon you add the tougher, and more brittle, the steel becomes. When you have a designation like 1020 mild steel, the 1000 series means it's a piece of steel not iron or aluminum. The second, two-digit number indicates the percentage of carbon that's been added to the mixture. 10 and 20 are low percentages, what you commonly find with mild steel. With 1045 steel, the carbon content is higher which makes it tougher."

"Chrome-moly is actually a general term for the widely used medium-carbon steel. This material startes out as 1030 mild steel before they added chromium and molybdenum (thus the chrome-moly name). A common chrome-moly designation might be 4130, again the 4000 number indicates the general series and the rest of the numbers indi-

Building accurate frames requires very stout surface tables with strong brackets that ensure nothing moves during the set up or tack welding. C. Maida

A good frame comes with a well supported neck. Much of the stress and vibration experienced by a frame is concentrated here, thus the gusset. C. Maida

From Redneck Engineering comes this Bobber frame complete with curved mild steel tubing, set up to run a typical Evo, five-speed driveline. Note the interesting side bracket for the transmission.

cate exactly how much of the various alloys the metal contains."

"Chrome-moly tubing starts out as cold-rolled bar stock, which is formed into seamless tubing in the manner described above for mild steel. This is extremely high quality material at a good price. The strength (both tensile and yield) is two to three times that of mild steel. It comes with an additional designation: N is normalized, A is annealed."

"To create the N grade of chrome-moly the material is heated to a moderate temperature and then allowed to cool gradually under controlled conditions. This slow cooling is an invitation for all the molecules to line up and position themselves wherever they want. This ensures they haven't been forced or locked into a stressful situation like cars experiencing gridlock on the freeway.

Condition A is more of the same, to the point where much of the toughness of the material is lost. With condition A chrome-moly you have to re-heat-treat the material after the welding or manufacturing is finished. Most of the chrome-moly that's sold is condition N, a tough material that doesn't need to be heat treated after the welding or forming."

"The big advantage of using mild steel is the inexpensive cost. This material can be welded and formed easily and almost anybody can do the work."

"Chrome-moly on the other hand is harder to weld but it has a very high strength-to-size ratio. You can use a smaller piece of tubing that weighs less to do the same job. The downside to chrome-moly is the poor availability and higher cost. And all the welds must be TIG welds. You cannot wire-feed weld chrome-moly. With 'moly the parts must fit precisely, you can't fill a gap with weld material, it makes for a really ugly, really weak, weld."

THE VERY IMPORTANT MOCK-UP

The importance of doing a thorough and complete, as opposed to a quick and dirty, mock-up of the bike can't be over-emphasized. Shortcuts taken during the mock-up process will come back to haunt you a hundred times. Time taken here to do a good job will pay big dividends as the machine goes together smoothly during the final assembly without the need to go backwards and fix a problem that should have been identified during the mock-up.

Experienced shops build their custom motorcycles twice. Once while the major parts are still in their raw, unfinished state and once for real. The reasons for doing a mock up of the bike with raw components are numerous. First, you get to see how the bike is actually going to look. By bolting on the tank(s), fender and seat you

At the Donnie Smith Custom Cycles shop they like to have everything in place before they tear the bike apart for paint. They go so far as to determine where all the electrical components go and whether or not any small brackets are needed.

1-3/8" tubing and a 35 degree rake are found on this Rolling Thunder Softail frame. A 200mm rear tire can be mounted into the swingarm along with your choice of shock absorbers. Biker's Choice/Rolling Thunder

Another Redneck product, this Un-Bagger is available as either a rolling chassis or a finished machine.

can see how the bike looks and whether or not you like the new lines and the way all the components work together in a visual sense. This requires that you set up the bike at ride height, and that your work area is large enough to get back from the bike far enough to see it as you will when it's parked outside. If the garage is small you might put the work bench on wheels or roll the mock up outside so you can be back far enough to make honest judgments about the lines and proportions of the parts.

Perhaps more important than being able to see how the bike looks, is the check to see how the various components actually fit the frame and work together. This is the time to weld brackets to the frame or enlarge a hole in the fender so it bolts correctly to the strut. You don't want to discover the need for a bracket or new hole after all the parts come back from the paint shop.

Part of checking the fit of all the parts includes a thorough examination to ensure that when the suspension moves through the full range of motion, especially when it bottoms, that fenders and brackets can't possibly touch the tires. Remember that when you bottom the bike on a rough road the suspension probably moves slightly past what appears to be the "stop." The best builders and fabricators anticipate a worst-case scenario by using

A majority of custom bikes are still built on this time-proven soft-tail, five-speed platform. Engine and tranny are bolted separately to the frame, so moving one component doesn't have to affect the position of the other.

smooth button-head fasteners under the fender that screw up or away from the rubber to mount the fender. This method ensures that if contact is made the rubber only finds a smooth surface, and not a rough edge to grind against.

At the risk of repeating the obvious, we all like to see fenders set down close to the tire. The only problem, besides those already mentioned, is the fact that tires grow in size as speed increases, thus diminishing the clearance. At the Donnie Smith shop they like to use a broken drive belt as a spacer between tire and fender during mock-up to ensure clearance between rubber and metal. Flexible tubing can be used as well.

Finally, don't miss the obvious trouble areas. Make sure the clips on the inside of some fenders, intended to hold the taillight wires, can't touch the side of tire, and that the tire can't touch the bolt or pin assembly used to hold down the back of the seat (many builders now use Velcro or suction cups).

OFFSET DRIVETRAINS

Installing a fat tire in an existing bike or frame, or designing a frame to accept a 200 or bigger tire, often involves offsetting the transmission, or transmission and engine, to the left. The basic problem is that as rear tires get wider they inevitably run into the drive belt.

To create some clearance between the new tire and the belt you either have

Because the Twin Cam drivetrains combine the engine and transmission into one unit, the wide tire kit extends the mainshaft so the drive pulley is farther outboard. Then a series of spacers are used to move the inner primary outboard as well.

The Evo, five-speed drivetrain uses wide tire kits as shown (in various dimensions), with a spacer between the engine and inner primary, and another to move the compensator sprocket outboard, and (in some cases) an offset transmission mounting plate. Most modern frames now have transmission offset built in.

to move the tire/wheel to the right, or the belt to the left. Sometimes you can move the tire to the right slightly by taking metal off the caliper carrier or spacer that locates the right side of the wheel, then add a spacer of that same dimension between the inside of the pulley and the left side of the rear wheel. This is done with factory frames and will often allow the use of tires one or two sizes bigger than what came on the bike. Most people however, want a rear tire more than one or two sizes bigger than stock, and that means somehow moving the belt to the left, which in turn means offsetting the transmission. An old school option might involve using a drive chain in place of the belt as an easy way to create a bit more clearance.

Offsetting the transmission requires a short discussion of the drivetrain on a typical hardtail or soft-tail style frame. While the new TC 88 motors use an essentially unitized engine and transmission, the earlier non-rubber-mount Evo engines used in Softails connect to the transmission only on the left side through the inner and outer primary and the primary drive itself. What this means is that it's relatively easy to keep the engine

in the center of the frame, and offset the transmission to the left (though some frames offset the engine and the transmission).

When people first started adding wire tires, they often used a "Wide Tire Kit." This consisted of a spacer between the left side of the engine and the inside of the inner primary, an offset transmission mounting plate, and a spacer for the compensating sprocket.

This kit and many like it, effectively move the transmission over from 1/4 to a full inch. As the belt steps farther and farther to the left though, it eventually hits the frame. Creating room for the belt can be done with a re-designed swingarm, or a frame created specifically to allow the use of a huge rear tire and belt drive. The problem that arises from moving the transmission, and the primary drive with clutch assembly, farther and farther over is the effect all that weight has hangin' out on the left side. This is not static weight, but spinning weight with its own gyroscopic effect.

It's not that you can't offset the transmission, or the engine and transmission on a rubber-mount Evo-powered bike. It's just that there's a limit to how far to the left you can push all that weight before new problems arise.

Moving Unitized Engines and Transmissions

TC 88 engines and transmissions, and earlier rubber mount FXR and Dyna engines and transmission are bolted together as a unit. When a "wide" tire was only a 180 or 200, most builders would offset both the engine and transmission to the left slightly with offset mounts. With the advent of 250 and wider tires you can find a variety of new-style offset transmission kits on the market. Intended for Dyna drivetrains with super wide tires,

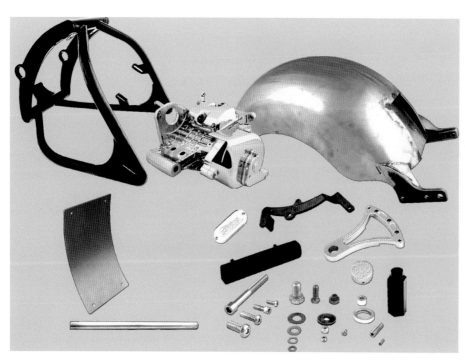

From Xtreme Machine comes this 300 tire kit designed to put some really fat rubber on the rear of that factory Softail. Includes RSD transmission, swingarm, fender, hardware and the wheel of your choice.

these kits move the inner primary and the primary drive to the left with spacers (and a longer main-shaft for the transmission). Instead of moving the entire transmission to the left, this kit simply moves the clutch assembly and output pulley to the left. The net effect is a final drive pulley located one inch farther to the left to clear the latest in ultra-wide rubber.

RIGHT HAND DRIVE

As discussed above, wider and wider tires typically mean transmission and drivetrain offsets farther and farther to the left. The solution to ever-expanding offsets is a right hand drive transmission. Baker, JIMS, Rivera and Prowler, to mention only a few, build five and six-speed transmissions with right hand drive. By moving the final drive to the bike's right side (these are big twins, not Sportsters) you eliminate the need to use spacers to move the primary drive and transmission to the left. The result is a more balanced motorcycle.

As Bert Baker of Baker Drivetrain explains: "The right side drive is evolutionary. Now you don't have the transmission set way over on the left side, and the engine drive sprocket isn't spinning way out there an inch or more away from the case. It creates a balanced motorcycle."

Obviously, the RSD tranny will only work with a chassis specifically designed to accept the right hand drive transmission.

This is it, the proverbial left-side-drive, five-speed transmission, in a soft-tail style case.

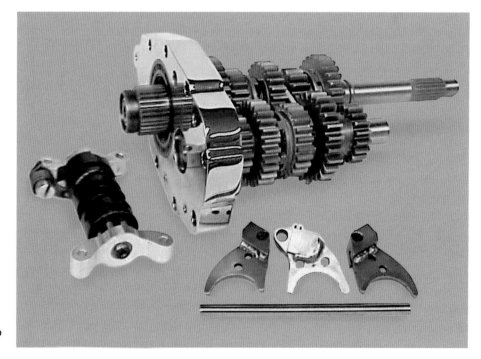

Baker makes this right hand drive gear set to allow you to transfer your belt to the opposite side of your chassis for improved balance. Biker's Choice/Baker Drivetrain

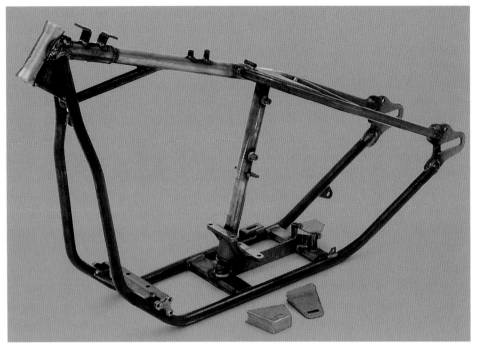

Using an old school wishbone design, Paughco sells their chopper style frame complete with a 2-1/4" stretch and 10 degree rake. Biker's Choice/Paughco

CHOOSE A FRAME

Please note: This is an overview of the market, not a buyer's guide, and does not include every frame and swingarm. To achieve that goal, the book would be about 500 pages long.

Hardtails:

There are a number of interesting alternatives for builders seeking these very simple frame designs. In addition to rake angles, you can buy your hardtail frame "stretched" in either – often both – dimensions. Some hardtails come with a "wishbone" shape in the front downtubes, and some provide for rubber-mounted engines. A few of these frames mimic the dimensions of the early Harley-Davidson frames, like the hardtail frames from Jammer and others. Most of the modern hardtails will accept any Big Twin engine including the new TC 88B. New designs with wider rear sections allow you to use the currently popular 250 and 300 rear tires with belt drive.

With the current popularity of old skool bikes, a number of companies offer frames with a traditional look, setup to run a four-speed transmission, and a narrow rear tire.

While the traditional hardtail frame includes the welded in center post between the engine and transmission, newer designs delete that post (or use a bolt-in post) a necessity for any chassis that accepts the unitized TC 88 engine and

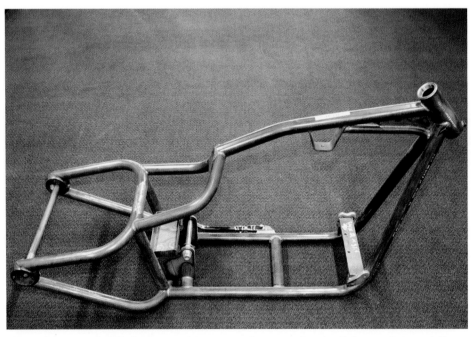

From Motorcycle Works comes this extremely strong hardtail frame designed for Evo or TC engines with Dyna transmission. Made from .156 and .188 inch wall, large diameter tubing, this chassis can be ordered for RSD or LSD in nearly any rake and stretch dimension.

transmission from H-D. As mentioned elsewhere a TC 88 engine (the non-B version) can be mated up to an earlier style five-speed transmission with the used of an adapter plate on the back of the engine.

Twin Shock

Though for many years there were only a few of these designs to choose from in the aftermarket, today every major catalog has at least one new twin-shock frame available in a number of configurations. Most of these frames will accept any Big Twin engine and many will accept a four, five or six-speed transmission. Like the modern soft-tail style frames, many manufacturers of twin-shock frames make a few models that will accept an extra-wide rear tire.

You can still buy a twin-shock frame that bolts the Big Twin engine solid to the frame, matched up to your choice of transmission. Many of these are similar to older H-D designs and will not accept the massive rear tire. A few are even designed to run a drum rear brake.

Years ago the folks in Milwaukee discovered that by suspending the engine and transmission in rubber, the vibrations of two 3-1/2 inch pistons could be isolated from the rider. Many aftermarket frames use the isolation system designed originally for the FXR series of motorcycles. Chopper Guys, distributed by CCI and Drag Specialties, offer

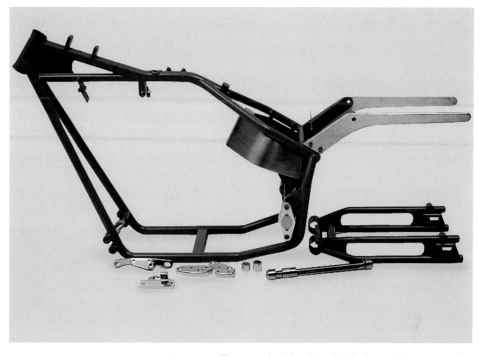

Daytec offers up the Skulker FXR frame for use with the rubber mount system and uses a 34 degree rake. Biker's Choice/Daytec

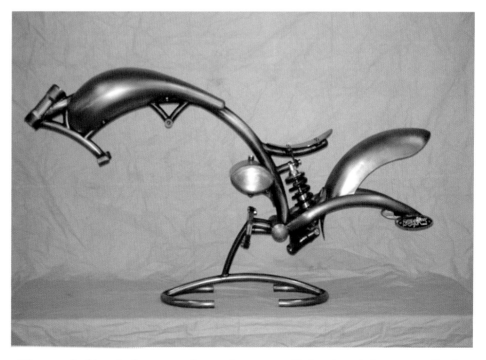

The trend of late is from two downtubes to one. Redneck took it one step further and eliminated the downtube all together. Designed to accept a Buell drivetrain.

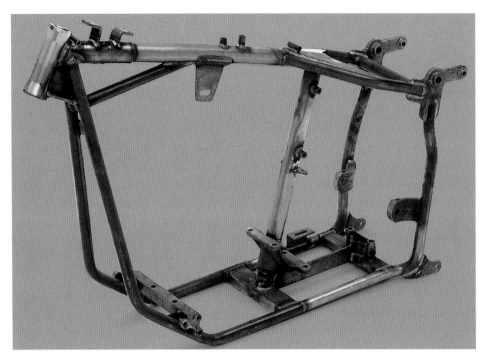

When trying to build a bike that carries the look of the Super Glide in its genes, the straight leg swingarm model from Paughco fills the bill. Biker's Choice/Paughco

more than just an FXR-type suspension system. They offer complete FXR frames very similar to those built in Milwaukee. With an extra two inches of backbone stretch, an offset kit for the unitized engine and transmission, and a wider swingarm the frames are ready for the new millennium and the mandatory 180 rear tire.

Like all other parts of this market, the twin-shock frames are evolving rapidly from the traditional designs many of us grew up with to more exotic forms. If you think the only way to have a really wide rear tire is with a soft-tail or hardtail frame, consider the offerings from Arlen Ness. Their Y2K frame is based on Dyna engine and transmission supports, and comes with a rear section wide enough for a 300 tire. Because the oil tank is under the transmission, the seat is right down there on the pavement.

SOFT-TAIL STYLE FRAMES

By far the most popular frame ever conceived for a V-Twin engine is the one that looks like a hardtail while providing a moderate amount of suspension travel. The best of both worlds you might say, the soft-tail frame bolts the engine and transmission directly into the frame and provides the clean lines that only a hardtail can offer.

Prior to the introduction of the TC 88 engine, nearly all soft-tail style frames used a center post,

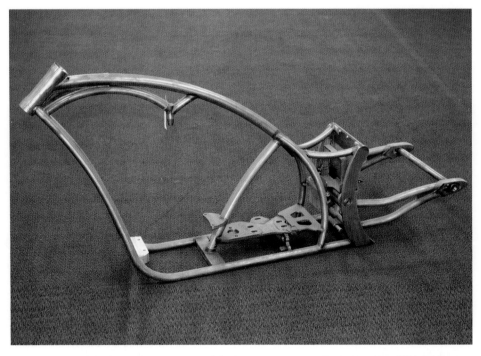

From Legends comes this long Lowlife frame guaranteed to put your fanny close to the ground. Narrow bottom frame rails mean minimal dragging in corners despite the low stance.

Legalities and EPA Compliance

MSOs and Titles

When you buy a frame, engine cases, or a complete engine from any legitimate aftermarket supplier you will get an MSO (Manufacturers Statement of Origin). This paperwork is essential if you want to get a title for your new motorcycle. Be sure MSOs are filled out correctly and that any previous transfers are noted. Before providing a title for any home-built or reconstructed bike most states insist that you provide them with the MSO with serial numbers noted for both the engine cases and the frame.

Don't buy parts unless they're legal and come with good paperwork. To break this rule is to risk a hassle with the state when you have the bike registered. When it comes time for registration, the state will want to see receipts for all the parts you purchased. Partly so they know the sales tax is paid and partly so they know they aren't stolen. Many states require you to bring the finished bike to a DMV station or highway patrol officer for an inspection.

In the case of a donor bike mated with a new frame, you need the MSO for the new frame, and the title and bill of sale for the donor bike. Each state is a little different, so it pays to call and ask for the guidelines. Also be sure to include all the items required for a motorcycle in your state, i.e. lights, horn and turn-signals. The best advice on getting through this process comes from shops that regularly build bikes, they know the drill. It's also a good idea to use the same DMV or inspection station that a busy shop does, simply because the people who work at that facility are accustomed to dealing with motorcycles and the paperwork involved in a reconstructed vehicle.

The EPA Situation

For the past couple of years we've all heard the horror stories about how the EPA planned to make custom bikes illegal. To paraphrase Mark Twain, the rumors of the industry's death have been greatly exaggerated. The EPA did adopt the letter of understanding with the aftermarket industry, dated July, 25, 2006 (see www.mic.org - look under the V-Twin category). To oversimplify: various engine companies, including S&S and TP Engineering, offer EPA compliant engine packages that come with a sticker you can apply to the bike which makes it EPA legal - as long as you don't tamper with the engine, and you use an exhaust system with the required amount of back pressure. Compliant engine packages can be used by individuals or shops to build bikes that are EPA legal. These bikes will still be required to meet all the standard legal requirements for a motorcycle in the state in which they are licensed. Individuals can still build a one-in-a-lifetime EPA exempt bike using a non-compliant engine package.

The Real World

Squiggy from dumbassbikers.com, a man who sells engines and engine packages all day over the 'net, tells us that the only states currently enforcing the EPA rules are California and New York, but of course that situation could change. The good news is the simple fact that you can indeed build a totally legal motorcycle, one that's legal and complaint now and five years from now. For more information on the local situation, contact the local shops and ask whether the bikes they build have to be compliant. The MRF (Motorcycle Riders Foundation) web site is also very informative: www.mrf.org.

Insurance

Whether or not you can get full coverage for your bike still depends mostly on your agent. Some will insure the bike for little more than a Harley, others want an extra thousand dollars. In Minnesota we have good luck with both Great Northern Insurance and a local American Family agency (see Sources), both offices have agents licensed in other states.

None of this legal information is meant to discourage you, people build fully legal bikes every day in every state, but there are a couple of speed bumps which can be avoided, or negotiated, if you check them out ahead of time.

and bolted the engine to two pads located ahead of the post, and the transmission to similar pads behind the post (with an additional bracket on the transmission's right side). Daytec was one of the first to install a plate for transmission mounting, instead of two pads, thus strengthening the frame.

Many of these soft-tail style frames come with the transmission mounting holes already offset, eliminating the need for an offset plate, and a wider rear section and matching swingarm, to accommodate the ten inch rubber we all take for granted.

ALTERNATIVE DESIGNS

There are a few frames on the market with hidden shock absorbers that do not follow the configuration of a standard soft-tail style frame. Some put the shocks at the top of the tri-angulated swingarm, under the seat. In this way the shocks compress when the suspension first hits a bump, like they do on a twin-shock frame. And as mentioned elsewhere, some "soft-tail" frames use a simple tubular swingarm, as opposed to the typical triangulated swingarm more typically used on soft-tails, supported by shocks placed under the transmission.

SWINGARMS

Fat Tires for Skinny Frames

You don't have to buy a complete "fat-drive" frame in order to run a wide rear tire. The aftermarket does supply extra wide swingarms that allow you to mount 250 and 300 series tire in a factory Softail frame, or a 200 or 250 tire in a factory Bagger.

For Baggers, both Klock Werks and FBI (Fat Baggers Inc) offer kits that put a 250 or 300 tire in a stock Bagger frame. In addition to the new wheel and tire, the kits come with a swingarm and rear fender.

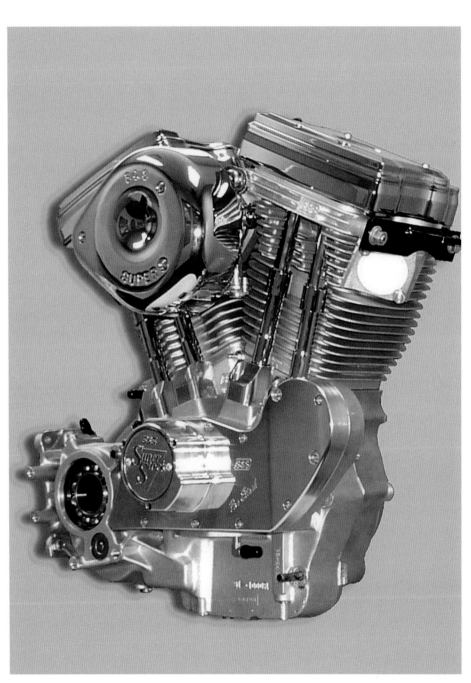

With all the custom-building focused on Big Twins, it's easy to forget the lighter and more compact Sportster drivetrain. If you're not happy with a 1200 HD motor or a Buell powerplant, consider a complete 91 or 100 inch engine from S&S.

34

Harley-Davidson even has a kit that allows you to run a wider rear tire in a late model Softail chassis. There are actually two kits, for pre and post-2000 model Softails that allows the owner to swap the stock 130 series rear tire for a 150 series tire from Dunlop. These kits create the necessary clearance between belt and tire through the use of a narrower belt and appropriate rear pulley.

Many of the wheel companies offer a kit that allows the installation of a 250 or 300 tire in a stock Softail, either Evo or Twin Cam. PM sells a Phatail kit complete with 18X8.5 inch wheel and fender that allows the fat rubber to rest comfortably in the confines of a bone-stock HD frame. Another high quality company normally associated with wheel and brake components, RC Components, also makes a complete line of wide tire kits. Not to be outdone by the competition, Xtreme Machine has their own 300 tire kit seen in a nearby illustration. All of these kits require you

If you want a Shovel that will keep up with the latest Evos and TCs, try this 103 inch alternator engine with 5 inch stroke and 3-5/8 inch bore. Jammer

to eliminate the stock fender struts and start over with their fender, swingarm and wheel. If you're looking to add a wider tire to an older Softail, most professional shops can get a 200 tire in a stock Softail and keep the stock swingarm, though (again) the fender struts have to go.

ENGINES, WHICH ONE BEST FITS YOUR NEEDS

A look through the current issue of Hot Bike or American Iron magazine will demonstrate one fact: There are more engine choices than ever before. Without delving into the land of Shovelheads, Knuckleheads or other more exotic choices, what follows is a simplified look at your options when it comes time to choose the engine for that new scratch built bike.

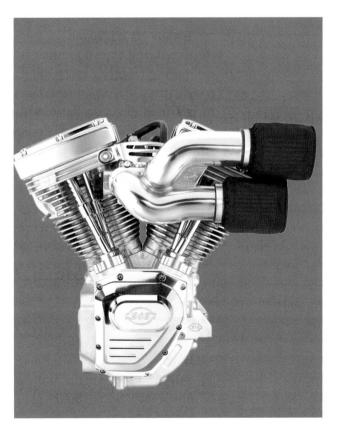

Complete 124 inch Twin Cam engines are available from S&S in either plain aluminum or polished finish, carbureted or fuel injected. S&S claims nearly 130 hp with a carburetor.

EVO

Evo-style engines are offered in every size and power rating you can imagine. A discussion of the Evo must include the original 80 inch example from Milwaukee. With all the lights and cameras focused on the big block examples from the aftermarket, it's easy to forget what a good, and durable engine the original Evo is. In what we used to call "hot rod 80" form these engines put out an easy 80 horsepower and 80 foot pounds of torque, with plenty of that power available relatively low in the RPM range where most of us ride. With more compression and camshaft these engines can be nudged over 100 horses. That's plenty of horsepower for a light custom bike or Bobber.

The Evo engine is still available new from the factory, and at very good prices. For a budget bike-building project, a factory Evo is one of the best values out there. At dumbassbiker.com (we didn't make that up) you can have a natural finish 80-inch Evo for $2795 without carb or intake manifold.

Good values are also offered by RevTech (Custom Chrome), Midwest and Ultima to mention just a few. When you're ready to step up to the bar and order off the top shelf, companies like S&S and TP Engineering offer Evo engines in displacements that start in the low 100s and go all the way to 145.

TWIN CAM

For all those riders who want to power their new bike with the latest offering from Milwaukee, complete TC 88 engines are available from your local dealer, in both A and B form. Again, these can be found at outlets like dumbassbiker.com,

At Ultima you can have a complete drivetrain package. From a 107 in black and silver with a 5-speed, to a 140 fully polished with a 6-speed. EPA compliant engines and packages are available as well. Ultima.

Though the new motors have enough power to break a belt, the 1-1/2 inch version is still found on many custom-built bikes. The longevity depends a lot on the rider!

as well as your local dealer. You can even buy the 103 inch Screamin' Eagle version of the TC engine. Though it took a while for the aftermarket to offer TC engines, new 120 inch TC engines, A or B are available from JIMS, and S&S offers their own 124 inch TC engine complete with Super G carb or the S&S fuel injection system.

Many of the frame manufacturers offer their most popular chassis in various configurations to match the engine of your choice. Rolling Thunder, for example, states that all their frames, "Can be ordered for Twin Cam A or B." Because the Twin Cam engines interlock with the transmission, there is no conventional boss on the back of the engine, like on an Evo, to bolt the back of the engine to the frame. To install an A motor into an Evo frame it's necessary to simply install an adapter on the back of the motor. This provides the necessary mounting points on the back of the powerplant. There may be a slight clearance problem between the new adapter and the frame's center post, nothing that can't be resolved through the judicious use of a four-inch grinder.

The A motor installed in such a fashion into an Evo frame can be matched up to a five or six-speed pre-2000 soft-tail style transmission. Essentially you have an Evo-style drive train in an Evo frame with a TC motor for power.

The B motor can't be so easily adapted to an Evo Frame. First, there's the problem of the center post, still found on many aftermarket frames. Then there's the front motor mount. What separates a B motor from an A motor are the counterbalancers and drive system. This means the cases, and front motor mounts, have to be changed to accommodate the weights and the chain drive.

The front motor mount is more like a tube cast into the case that hangs on an "axle". What all this means is that Twin Cam B engines need to be used as a unit with the matching transmission and installed into a chassis designed for the B engine.

WHICH ONE

Trying to decide which engine to install in that new frame is a bit of a dilemma. Both are excellent engines, it will come down to personal opinion, style and budget. A complete factory Evo engine is a heck of a value. If you look only at power per dollar the various aftermarket Evos are hard to beat

Before leaving the topic we should mention that because a number of riders are replacing 80 inch Evos with much bigger aftermarket engines, there are some really good deals to be had on complete pre-driven Evo mills. Before snapping up that great deal, remember that the motor isn't worth a damn without the right paperwork. Rules vary state by state (see Title Considerations in Chapter One), but it's not a good idea to buy any engine unless you have an MSO, or proof of legal ownership, that will satisfy the authorities in your state.

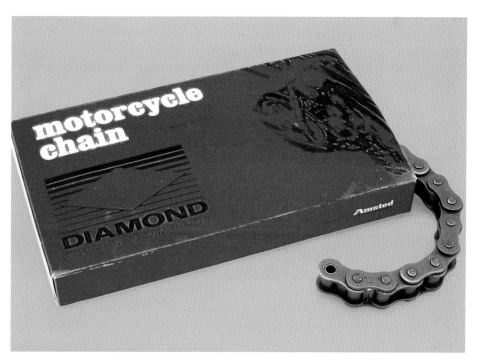

Used on metric rockets in the 1970s, a good 530 chain is a very durable piece of power-transmitting equipment. O-rings lock in the factory lube so they're not as messy as in the old days. You can even get them with plated side plates.

Available from American Thunder in Minnesota, this rolling chassis kit uses a variation on the Ness Y2K frame. Kit and frame are available in various dimensions.

USE A DONOR BIKE

We should also mention, for the benefit of anyone building a complete bike, that the price of used bikes is down. This means it might make good sense financially to buy a complete bike and then use the drivetrain, wheels, some of the sheet metal and whatever else you can adapt, to build the new motorcycle. If you look at the price of a new engine with transmission and primary drive, the idea of a donor bike looks better and better. Not to sound like a broken record, but you need to check ahead of time to see if you will be able to register the new bike, created by combining most of one existing motorcycle, with a new frame and various other components.

The donor bike concept started back in the original Chopper days when a person could take their compete Panhead or Shovel, order a new hardtail frame from one of the many mail-order houses, and then install most of the original components, including wheels and sheet metal, in and on the new frame. Today, companies like Redneck Engineering and Motorcycle Works build neat little Bobber frames designed to accept Buell or Sportster drivetrains, wheels, forks and even the gas tank. With the price of used bikes at an all time low, the donor bike concept could easily be employed when building a big-twin powered machine.

The streetster rolling kit from Paul Yaffe, can be purchased ready for an Evo or Twin Cam B motor, and rear tires up to 250 wide. Comes with 60-spoke wheels and one of two possible rear fenders. PYO

Take a look at the price of Evo-powered Softails from Milwaukee, or some of the non-Harley bikes for that matter. Buy the right bike, pick the correct frame, skip the expensive goodies, add your own labor and you can have a very nice bike for a lot less than if you went out and bought all the components new.

WIDE BELTS, NARROW BELTS & CHAINS

Harley-Davidson discovered years ago that a toothed belt is the ideal way to transfer power from the transmission's output sprocket to the rear wheel. Installation of the belt drive combines the efficiency of a chain without the mess or maintenance. Up until the introduction of the 2000 models the Big Twins used a 1-1/2 inch belt while the Sportster line used a 1-1/8 inch belt. The larger belt held up well in day to day service and would withstand considerable abuse without stripping or breaking.

Things have changed however. First, starting with the 2000 models, most factory Softails and Dynas use a reinforced version of the 1-1/8 inch belt. This was done primarily to make room for larger rear tires. Second, new big-bore aftermarket engines of 113 and 121 cubic inches commonly make 130 or more horsepower. These monster motors have the power to break 1-1/2 inch belts like they're rubber bands.

In the last few years a lot of bikes are showing up with a chain in place of the belt. A good 530 chain is stronger than a belt, and chains leave more room for fat tires, make it easy to change final drive ratios, and come with O-rings to lock in the factory lube. Order yours with nickel plated side plates for a nice look. Instead of that nasty chain lube we grew up with (some of us at least) modern riders often lube the chain with nothing nastier than silicone spray which keep the O-rings compliant.

You don't have to run a chain, belts work fine, even when transmitting the power of a big engine. A lot of this depends how you drive and even how much you weigh. So first you have to decide if you have room for the belt, second, if a belt is going to be durable enough for your powerplant and riding style.

KITS, KITS, KITS

The hot ticket in frames isn't just the frames themselves, but rather the components that come along with the chassis and swingarm. Everyone from Dave Perewitz to American Thunder and Paul Yaffe offer rolling frame kits. By buying the frame with the wheels and sheet metal you know what the profile of the bike is. You know essentially what it's going to look like. You also eliminate some of the hassles of building a bike, things like: how long should the fork tubes be, who can weld on the tank and fender mounts? You can even get some of the kit manufacturers to cut the wheel spacers for the rear wheel and make the job of drivetrain and rear wheel alignment much, much easier.

If you want that scratch-built bike long and low, try this Double Trouble frame with 7 inches of stretch in the backbone and a 4 inch dropped neck. Comes with 6 degree trees for good handling. PYO

Chapter Three

Suspension Components

Shocks and Springs

Some riders are willing to forgo comfort to be the coolest kid on the block, but many of us would prefer to have a modicum of comfort included in our travels. For all those who require a softer-tail we offer a look at those tubular components called shock absorbers.

TWO COMPONENTS COMBINED

Though the shocks absorbers used on most motorcycles combine hydraulics and springs into one unit (this happens even with the front fork) it's easier to understand how each works by looking at the components separately.

Whether it's an expensive outboard shock with adjustable valving, or a simple soft-tail design, nearly all "shocks" combine a spring with a damper unit.

Start with a spring that supports a weight. Compress the spring and let go. It doesn't just bounce back to its original position but rather goes well past that point and through a series of diminishing oscillations before coming back to the starting point.

If the springs in question are supporting your bike, the up and down movement is unpleasant to say the least. In order to dampen those oscillations a shock absorber (technically these are dampers not shocks) is used, often incorporated into the spring assembly. The first shock absorbers were just "friction" shocks rubbing a series of discs together to dampen the up and down movement of the springs. Friction shocks, however, exert the greatest resistance at the beginning of movement and then become easier to move once the "stiction" has been overcome. This is the exact opposite of the ideal characteristics found in a good damper unit. Hydraulic shocks are now standard equipment on all motorcycles. In place of friction between two discs, hydraulic dampers use the resistance of a non-compressible fluid to control the movement of the sprung portion of the shock absorber.

INSIDE THE SHOCK

Looking at a modern shock it's easy to imagine the piston attached to the pushrod, moving through a cylinder filled with oil. The viscosity of the oil, its quality and the size of the hole(s)

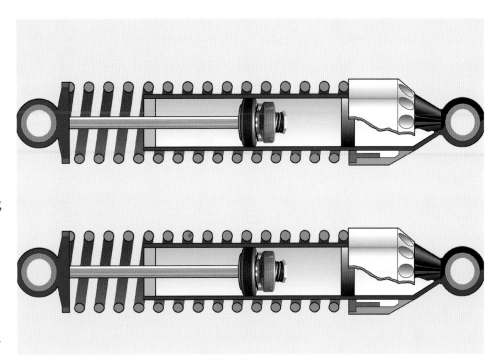

The technology found inside the 440 series shock from Progressive includes two individual damping circuits providing a high level of handling and comfort. Biker's Choice/Progressive Suspension

Even the least expensive soft-tail shocks are adjustable for preload, though you may have to take the shocks out of the bike to make the adjustment.

Q&A, Ted Tine

Ted, can you start by giving us some background, how did you come to manufacture shocks?

I used to race professionally in (SCCA) Trans-Am and (IMSA) Endurance Road Racing International Motorsports Association. Endurance racing, the likes of the 24 hours of Daytona and the 12 hours of Sebring. I worked for teams like Bruce Jenner, Paul Newman, Mazda, Lola, March, Porsche, Ferrari.

I started working on motorcycles as a hobby and then opened a professional shop. People who came by our booth at the shows always had questions about suspension, and complained that their bikes weren't handling well. So I took a set of popular dampers apart and found that the internals were very antiquated, nothing more than a car shock with a coil spring. Because of my background I figured I could design and build a better set of dampers for the motorcycling world. We introduced our first dampers in 1993-1994. About a year later we introduced our first set of 56mm inverted Forks and 46mm Right Side Up Forks along with other performance products. I was the first to design and offer a soft tail damper with a built in ride height and compression adjustment. These were all marketed under the Essex Motorsports name. Today these products are marketed under the Ted Tine Motorsports name.

What makes a good shock absorber or damper?

A quality damper is one that is designed specifically for the vehicle and the environment that it is to be used in - road racing, highway, etc. Quality also assumes that the damper is robust and meets the weight and costs targets. A good damper can also look cool and perform well. A good damper is engineered for each application. You need a good design, with high quality seals, and well designed bearing surfaces so the damper can perform well from a durability standpoint while maintaining high performance.

Always serious, Ted Tine is one of those guys who decided that if you want it done right, you have to do it yourself.

Q&A: Ted Tine

What kinds of adjustments are available in a quality shock for the street?

Adjustments don't necessarily make a quality product. The type and quantity of adjustments should be a function of the vehicle requirements. If an adjustment is necessary then the adjustment mechanism should be predictable, repeatable and somewhat linear over its adjustment range. It should also be as robust as possible. Typical adjustments include: Compression and rebound, which slows down or speeds up the piston or shaft as it moves through the oil inside the damper. And then you have spring preload, which also changes the ride height. And you have a ride height adjustment.

With soft tail frames do all the manufactures use the same dimensions and frame geometry?

Absolutely not. It seems today with the world of customizing being so popular it is possible to have anything from a single sided swingarm to your conventional type swingarm. Herein is where I think people get lost by forgetting the basic geometry of a chassis. They tend to move pick up points to lower or raise the bike, and in the end that change screws up the geometry, which in turn affects the ride and handling of the bike. Therefore frame manufacturers and builders should set up a chassis statically and measure all of the pick up points and where the dampers will mount. Remember that the dampers cannot correct for a geometry problem.

Also, it is important to know the mass of the vehicle and the unsprung mass. What people don't realize on a soft tail frame, or any frame for that matter, if you start to move mounting points even a 1/4 inch it upsets the geometry. Also, if you extend the swingarm or move the axle centers it changes the geometry. The same problem exists for the FX-style frames. If you change the mounting points, in most cases it changes the angle of the shocks. If you don't have the correct angle on the FX chassis you will have extension and rebound problems. The shock is designed for a specific geometry and the physical application. If the frame manufacturer recommends stock soft tail shocks the suspension geometry should be exactly the same as a stock factory Softail.

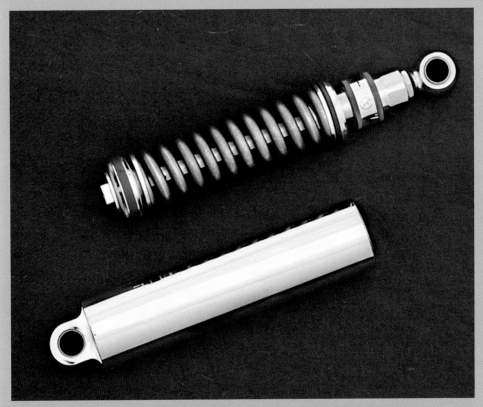

There is more inside a good shock absorber than most of us realize. Saving money on shocks is a bad idea, as they're so essential to the way the bike rides and handles.

In the case of high-quality outboard shocks the springs can be purchased as separate units.

The H-D air shocks used on stock Baggers come in two lengths. The shorter examples drop the bike roughly an inch.

that it passes through are the major factors affecting the stiffness of a particular shock absorber. Though the concept is simple, the actual innards of most modern shock absorbers are very sophisticated.

Most companies want different amounts of damping on compression and rebound. The two valves are very different, designed with very different characteristics in mind.

UNSPRUNG WEIGHT AND SHOCK ABSORBERS

At this point we need to back up and discuss sprung and unsprung weight, terms you're likely to see if you pick up a book or article about suspension design for nearly any vehicle. It's also a factor you should consider when trying to decide which shocks, brakes and wheels to buy. Most of the motorcycle, which is the frame, engine, sheet metal and all the rest, are considered sprung weight: weight supported by the springs. The wheels and tires, lower fork, and brake components, on the other hand are considered unsprung weight.

Consider a motorcycle running down the road. It hits a sharp bump in the pavement which forces the wheel up while compressing the spring. One of the goals of any good suspension system is to keep the tires on the pavement. When the bump in question drops away quickly you want the wheel to change direction rapidly and stay in contact with the asphalt. Even today's wide rubber places a very small foot print on the pavement, and it's crucial to maintain that contact for safe and confident riding.

The problem (one of the problems) is the momentum of the wheel and tire, which makes them want to continue in an upward direction even after the pavement is falling away. The compressed spring is trying to force apart the wheel and the frame. How much of the spring's energy raises the bike and how much of it forces the tire down to maintain its grip with the road depends on the ratio of sprung to unsprung weight.

A lighter wheel-tire-brake assembly will react more quickly to irregularities in the road while feeding less energy into the rest of the motorcycle.

You also have to consider the shock absorber's role in this scenario. To quote Doug from Koni: "Compression damping controls unsprung weight, how fast the wheel and brake assembly move up toward the rest of the bike. Rebound damping controls the sprung weight, the bike and rider. We only let you change the rebound damping, because the sprung weight is what you typically change between rides. You add a passenger, or you add gear, which changes the amount of sprung weight."

BUY QUALITY

As with every component on a modern bike, installing quality suspension components will ensure that the final assembly works as a whole. Cutting corners at any step in the process will negate this overall quality effort. Even shocks hidden from view should be of the finest quality or the ride and safety of the build will suffer.

Fluid friction provides the damping in a modern shock absorber. A shock that works hard on a bumpy road will heat up as the result of that friction. Inexpensive shocks allow air to mix with the oil, and the oil itself to change viscosity due to the heat. The net result is poor and inconsistent damping as the piston moves through an aerated froth of hot oil.

Inconsistent damping control and aerated oil are problems overcome by high quality shock absorbers. In a quality shock absorber all the components, from pistons to shafts, are larger and built to

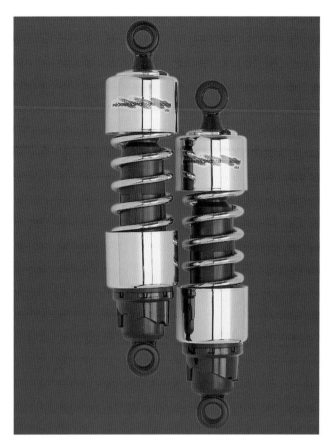

Sets of traditional coil over shocks are also sold by Progressive as we see in these 412 series models. Biker's Choice/Progressive Suspension

The 416 series of Magnumatic shocks from Progressive are sold to fit machines ranging from the Sportster to the big FLT and offer adjustability and easy installation. Biker's Choice/Progressive Suspension

When purchased with the chrome covers, the 412 series shocks take on a new appearance while providing the same qualities as their exposed cousins. Biker's Choice/Progressive Suspension

higher standards. The valves that control the damping are much more sophisticated to better handle a variety of road conditions and riding styles. To handle the heat, the amount of oil is increased. To diminish the heat the body of the shock is made of aluminum which aids in the dispersion of heat. To prevent aeration of oil the shock is gas-charged, or filled with premium oil that won't change viscosity.

WHAT TO BUY
Shocks for soft-tail type chassis

The shock absorber layout on a soft-tail type bike is much different than on a twin-shock bike. When you ride over a bump the shocks of the soft-tail type suspension get longer, not shorter. For this reason the rear suspension needs an external "bump stop" instead of making the shocks do the job of limiting suspension travel on compression. Usually there are two rubber bumpers under the seat that provide a stop to the swingarm's travel.

Consider too that Softails have less total travel than most twin-shock frames before lowering. There is one thing the technicians from all the shock manufacturing companies agree on: As you reduce travel you make the shock's job, providing suspension control and a good ride, harder and harder.

FITMENT

Softails from Milwaukee came with three slightly different rear suspensions. The first change came in 1989 and the next change came in 2000. Most current aftermarket frames use either the 1989 to 1999 or the 2000 and later shocks. The two designs are different enough (the earlier shocks use an eye on either end while the late-model shocks use a threaded bolt on the front end) that it would be tough to use or even buy the wrong one.

ANATOMY OF A SPRING

Compared to a shock absorber, a coil spring might seem the

The Texas chopper from American IronHorse features a soft-tail style suspension in a cleverly disguised configuration.

simplest thing in the world. There is however, more to a quality spring than meets the eye. Coil springs are rated in weight/distance. For example, how many pounds of force does it take to compress the spring one inch? You could take the coil springs out of your fork and test their ratings with a ruler and a scale.

The simplest springs are linear in their strength. That is, if 200 pounds will compress the spring one inch, then 400 pounds will compress the same spring two inches (up to a certain limit of course). Some springs are said to be "progressive" meaning the coils are wound tighter on one end than the other, which essentially creates a spring with a variable rate (this is typically in the twin-shock part of the market). On soft bumps you compress only the more tightly wound coils. On harsh bumps those coils "coil bind" quickly leaving you with a spring that is essentially much stiffer and better able to handle the larger bump. Some manufacturers offer a dual-rate spring made up of two different springs. Small bumps compress both springs which provides a softer effective rate. When the shorter spring coil binds, the rate of the other spring kicks in.

They're more important than you might think. So think about your choice of shock absorbers and don't spend millions on the motor and tranny and then go cheap on the two assembles that dictate much of the bike's ride and handling characteristics.

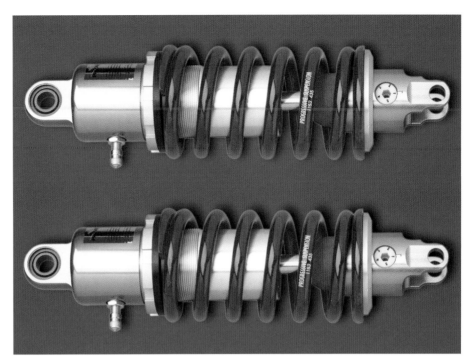

Some very high quality shocks offer the user the option of adjusting spring preload and damping, as well as internal pressure.

Biker's Choice sells these adjustable length rear shocks for use on 1989 through 1999 FXST and FLST chassis, simplifying one design choice. Biker's Choice

Chapter Four

The Fork

Form meets Function

Too many of us judge a fork assembly by the quality of the chrome plating, or the fact that a certain fork assembly might be "in style." While the fork remains a major visual component of the motorcycle, it also is required to be a functional piece as well. If you look at the types of forks being used even five years ago, and the forks available today, you see an explosion in styles and offerings compared to just a few years ago. Despite all the new entries in this field, the

When Dan Roche decided to build a new bike, he chose a Dragon model springer from American Suspension. Small, 4-1/2 inch, diameter headlight is from Headwinds.

largest group of available forks and components is still made up of OEM-style assemblies that are the same as or similar to those used on late model Harley-Davidson motorcycles.

TERMS

Wide-glide and narrow-glide refer to the distance between the two fork tubes. Because the aftermarket is dominated by parts intended to replace OEM pieces the discussion of fork assemblies must include fork offerings on current factory bikes. A factory wide-style fork, for example, measures nearly ten inches center-to-center (exact dimensions vary between the various Harley-Davidson models).

Hydraulic forks come in what we call "right side up" and upside down designs depending on whether the smaller diameter section of the fork tubes is held in place by the triple clamp or used to mount the front axle. In either case, the spring that holds up the front of the bike is inside each tube, as is the oil. Because of the oil and damper assembly, the fork is in essence both a spring and shock absorber.

With "upside down" designs, the larger diameter segment of each fork leg is bolted to the triple clamps. By clamping the larger diameter member to the triple trees, with only enough of the smaller diameter "piston" protruding to mount the axle and allow for suspension travel, the upside-down fork puts the strongest member in the triple trees - which reduces flex and makes for a more stable front end. This design also reduces unsprung weight by making the smaller diameter part of the fork the part that moves with the wheel over bumps.

Fork assemblies can be further divided according to how they dampen the

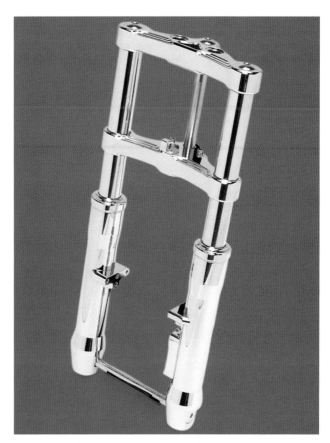

For the cycle that requires something a bit more stout, this fork assembly is available in 50mm. Biker's Choice

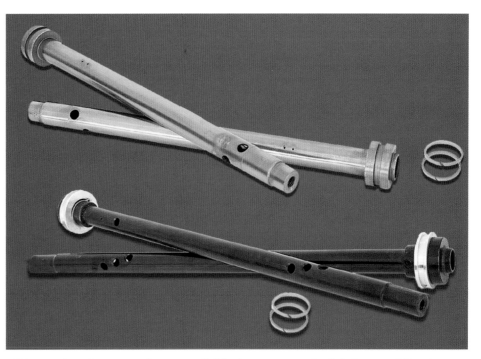

Aftermarket damper rods are available for most standard fork assemblies, but you're still expecting one set of holes to fit the needs of many types of bumps encountered at many different speeds.

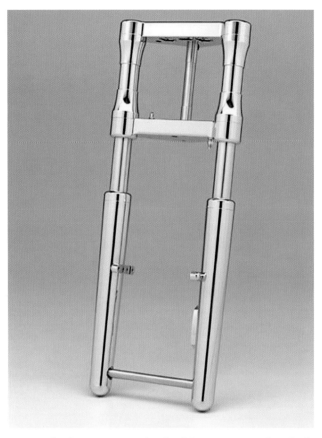

From the less-is-more school of design comes this sleek 41mm fork assembly. Cyril Huze

action of the springs. Many conventional OEM designs use damper rods. More sophisticated fork assemblies from both the aftermarket and Milwaukee are "cartridge style," with a separate damper inside the fork tube. Damper-rod forks use oil moving through fixed holes in the damper rods to do the damping. The biggest problem with these forks is trying to make one "hole" fit all situations. Big bumps encountered at high speed require large holes and minimal restriction, while smaller undulations in the pavement require smaller holes to provide any effective damping.

Cartridge forks use a cartridge to control the damping. Similar to high quality shock absorbers, these sophisticated assemblies use a different valve for rebound and compression, each with its own damping curve. This way the suspension engineer can design a fork with more damping action on rebound than on compression. These forks can be fairly stiff on small bumps without being too harsh on the larger ones, because the spring-loaded orifice changes size in response to the speed and the size of the bump you encounter.

Race Tech offers a Cartridge Fork Emulator. As Tom Hicks from Race Tech explained. These Gold Valve Emulators drop in on top of the damper rods. To install them you drill the compression holes in the damper rods pretty big so they don't do any damping. Now, on compression, the oil goes to the emulator, which uses a spring loaded valve to do the damping. The emulator makes the fork work more like one of the new cartridge style forks."

If you own a late-model Harley-Davidson and plan to replace the fork assembly or install a lowering kit,

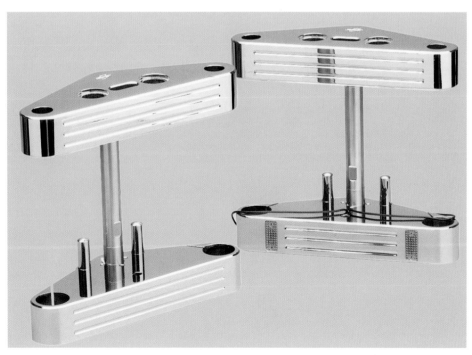

Triple trees come in every style and configuration imaginable, including these billet numbers with and without blinker lights. One of the advantages of using a standard size fork tube is the range of available trees. Biker's Choice

check first to see if the factory fork uses a cartridge, (like the V-Rod and later model Baggers for example). Don't be too quick to throw out the factory fork and/or cartridge for something sexier from the aftermarket that may not be nearly as sophisticated.

WHAT TO BUY

If you're looking for a good value in a complete hydraulic fork, look no further than a 41mm fork assembly. These forks come in three basic versions, FLT, Softail Custom and Heritage (also Fat Boy). The FLT (or Dresser) tubes are the shortest, with Heritage next in length and Softail Custom being the longest of all. Of course longer and (sometimes) shorter tubes are available in most styles from the various aftermarket companies. Or you can call Forking by Frank for a custom tube of any length.

If you want dual discs on a 41mm fork, you either have to run FL style lower fork legs with factory attaching points for the calipers, or use aftermarket lower legs like those from Arlen Ness, Custom Chrome, Drag Specialties or a dozen more.

The Deuce front end, which is technically a 41mm unit, can be ordered from the dealer of your choice, or a variety of aftermarket outlets. Buy yours as complete fork leg assemblies or a complete fork assembly, typically set up for a single disc.

LOWER LEGS AND FORKS

The aftermarket lower legs mentioned above provide one more way to dress up the front end of your bike. If you already have a conventional fork assembly, then the addition of billet lower legs might be another way to customize the fork assembly without the expense of a complete fork

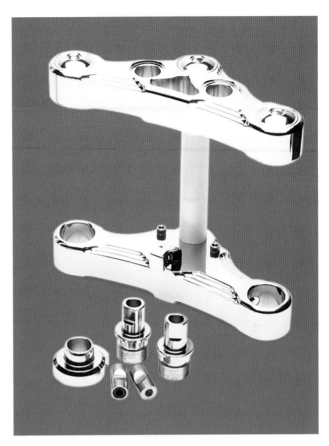

Biker's Choice brings us these 2 inch stepped triple trees in three configurations to best fit your design needs.

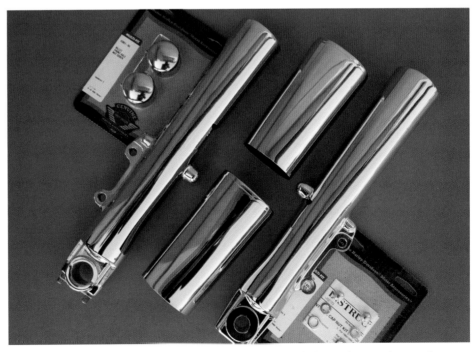

If your Hog came with polished, rather than plated, lower legs and cans these chrome upgrade kits are available at the dealership.

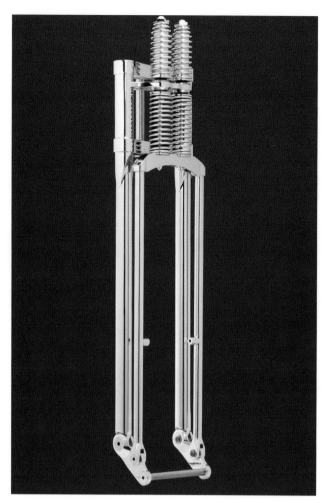

Rolling Thunder took our favorite fork, the springer, and redesigned it with improved geometry and better materials to ensure a supple ride and long life.

assembly. You can also buy chrome lower legs, with or without a complete chrome fork kit, for most factory models that came with polished rather than chrome fork assemblies. Again, these chrome lower legs can be purchased at the dealer or from the aftermarket. On the aftermarket side, you can combine billet lower legs of your choice with tubes and triple trees to put together a complete fork assembly.

Inverted forks were once the domain of companies like Storz, but today these designs are offered in various configurations by a large number of aftermarket manufacturers. In addition the factory offers inverted forks like the V-Rod units already mentioned.

SPRINGER FORKS

There's a wealth of new Springer forks available from a variety of companies, both new and old. Some builders go no father than their local dealer and use the factory springer, which is certainly a well-known and high-quality unit. Any springer fork you buy should have a means of controlling the oscillations and harmonics with shocks or some kind of shock absorber or damper.

Springer forks often make the triple trees an integral part of the fork assembly, so there's no easy way to adjust the trail, which is why Rolling Thunder offers two versions of their fork, one for frames with less than 33 degrees of rake and one for more radical frames with more than 33 degrees of rake. Redneck Engineering will simply manufacture the Springer for your particular

Though never as popular as the springer, the girder front end has certain functional advantages and can be manufactured to look old skool or new.

frame so both the length and trail are correct.

Many new Springer fork assemblies use a top tree drilled for conventional risers. Some come with an earlier-style top tree and accept traditional dog-bone style risers. Be sure you know which size axle your new Springer is designed to accept, so the wheel and fork are all on the same page. Many are designed for stock brakes and sheet metal and some do not. Ask the manufacturer which brakes are easiest to utilize in order to make things as easy as possible down the road.

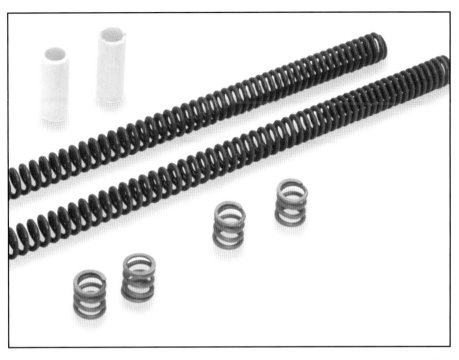

The better lowering kits use springs that are wound in a progressive fashion, (tighter coils at one end) so the spring rate gets gradually stiffer as it is compressed. Biker's Choice

GIRDER FORKS

A girder fork assembly is a much different animal than a springer. Modern Girders use a separate coil-over assembly, which means it's easy to adjust the spring tension, you can even change the entire coil-over assembly. Donnie Smith likes the design because, "they don't wind up when you hit the brakes hard like a springer." He likes the design well enough to recreate the girders he and brother Happy used to manufacture in the old Chopper days. Today, that fork is available from Custom Chrome as a signature Donnie Smith design.

AN INDIAN DESIGN

We can't leave the fork section without mentioning the newest old-skool fork, the leaf-spring design used on Indians of old. The complete affair, as manufactured by Kiwi Motorcycle Company, is available from the Jammer catalog, a great compendium of parts for anyone building a bike with a traditional flavor.

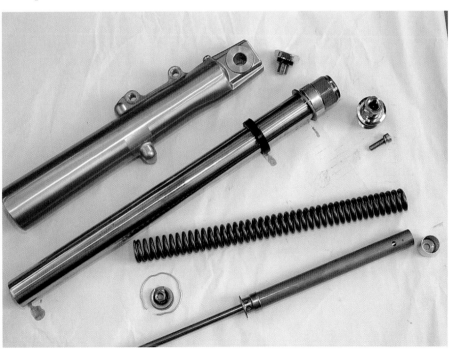

The completely disassembled left side fork tube assembly from a late model Bagger. Note the cartridge at the bottom.

Another pair of lower legs, this time with mounts for dual calipers.

WHAT FITS WHAT

The neck and fork stem bearings are the same on all late model Big Twins, Sportsters and nearly all aftermarket frames. In theory any triple tree should work on any frame. As many builders soon learn, there are always a few Murphy's-Law exceptions.

Some wide-glide trees don't work well on frames meant for narrow-glide forks, and the fork stop provisions on one frame might not match up to the stop-design used with a particular set of trees. One more thing, the distance between the centerline of the neck and the centerline of the tubes is not always the same, but should be considered because this dimension will affect the trail.

Like everything else, all the components that make up the front end of the bike must be designed (or modified) to work with all the other parts. A wide-style fork will require the right wheel hub and the right brackets or spacers to mount the front fender.

If you're building a bike from scratch, be sure to work through all these issues during the mock-up. Do the fork stops work, is the trail correct (see the trail illustrations in Chapter One) and is there enough clearance between the trees, bars, and the gas tank? When adjusting fork stops remember that if the bike goes over in the parking lot the force of the fall will likely force the bars past the normal end-of-travel which may push the bar into the gas tank. Custom sheet metal is nice, but better created in the shop, not at the local convenience store.

Johnny Legend went with a set of American Suspension inverted forks when building El Balla as well as adding 2 inches to their length.

Fork Assembly

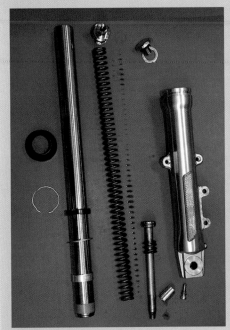

Here's a typical disassembled fork assembly from a late-model Softail. All work done at American Thunder.

Reassembly starts as Ken drops three top-out springs (for maximum lowering) and then the damper rod down into the fork tube.

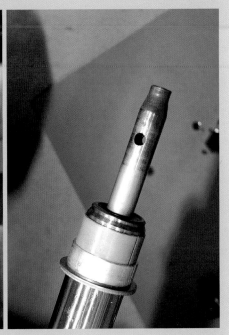

Here you can see the damper rod sticking out of the bottom of the fork tube.

The main spring is dropped into the tube next.

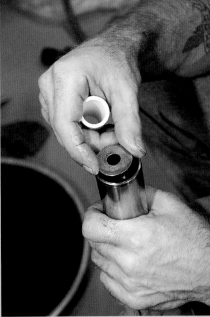

Followed by one of the washers that came with the kit.

Next in the assembly sequence: one more washer on top of the plastic sleeve (hard to see) and then the fork tube plug.

1. Now the lower stop goes on the damper rod...

FORK ASSEMBLY AT AMERICAN THUNDER

This little mini-assembly sequence took place at American Thunder in Savage, Minnesota. The fork being assembled is a stock 41 mm unit from a stock, 2005 Softail Standard, though the assembly of nearly any late model fork would be very similar to what you see here. The fork tube assemblies were disassembled so Ken could install a lowering kit which consisted of new main springs, top-out springs and pre-load spacers.

During the reassembly, Ken also installed new fork seals, and then refilled the tube assemblies with the required amount of fork oil.

3. After being coated with teflon sealer, the new sealing bolt and crush washer are inserted and tightened.

2. ...and the tube is inserted in the lower leg.

4. Next, the slider bushing and spacer are pushed down into the lower leg with the tool shown on the next page.

The tool shown is used to push (first) the slider bushing...

...and then the fork seal (inserted with the letters facing up)...

...into the lower leg as shown.

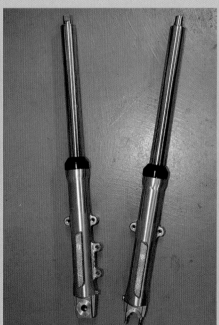

The snap ring and then the boot are the last two steps.

The result is two assembled fork tube assemblies.

Ken installs 12 ounces of 15 weight fork oil, the same amount and weight as stock.

Chapter Five

Brakes

Slow with the Go

We all like going fast, but at some point we will also need to slow down, and even stop our motorcycles. Whether it's for fuel, or flashing red lights in the mirrors, no one can ride forever.

It's hard to discuss brakes without a parallel discussion of physics. Brakes are basically heat machines. When you squeeze the lever the brake pads are forced against the spinning rotor which slows the motorcycle. In essence you are converting moving or kinetic energy into heat energy.

The aftermarket manufactures a vast array of high quality brake components, parts that are both beautiful and very functional. You do have to take care to correctly match the various parts of the brake system so they all work together to get you good, safe brakes.

KINETIC ENERGY

Kinetic energy is one of those non-linear relationships. A motorcycle traveling 60 miles per hour has four times (not two) the kinetic energy of the same machine at 30 miles per hour. Grabbing a handful of front anchor at 80 or 100mph means you're asking a lot of those brakes. It only makes good sense to buy the best components you can for that new motorcycle. The four-piston calipers offered by Harley-Davidson are quite good, way better than the old single piston units. In fact, anyone with the single piston units on their bike should upgrade at least the front wheel with the later factory calipers.

The nice thing about high quality brakes is the fact that they usually look as good as they work. Form generally follows function in this part of the market. The slickest calipers from Performance Machine or RevTech are extremely functional as well. When buying brakes for a high performance motorcycle, more is usually better. More rotor surface area, more pistons per caliper (usually with larger pads as well) and in some cases, more calipers. The down side to the "more brakes are better" theory is the expense, complexity and additional unsprung weight of more and bigger calipers.

Bill Gardner from GMA Brakes in Omaha, Nebraska offers an interesting insight into this whole business of buying high quality brakes. "When people buy good

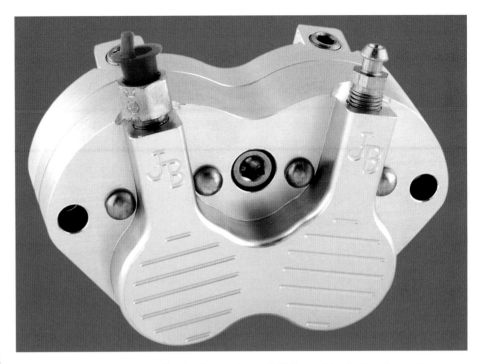

JayBrake makes a full line of individual braking components including their quad calipers that deliver better slowing power in an attractive package. Biker's Choice/JayBrake

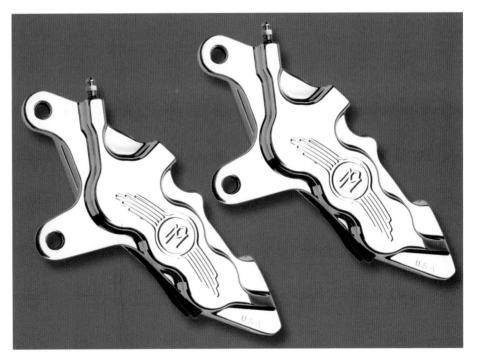

In most cases, more caliper pistons means better braking. The only downside is the additional cost of the caliper and possibly a small increase in weight. PM

brake components they do it to gain stopping ability, but they also gain something more subtle. They gain a better feel of what's going on, they gain confidence in their brakes and their ability to stop. It's called modulation."

The brake discussion here is limited to disc brakes. As you apply the brakes on a moving motorcycle weight transfers to the front wheel, which explains why the front wheel has at least seventy percent of the stopping power. Spend the bulk of your brake budget on the front wheel, it's the one with the most power to save your butt when that truck hooks a left turn in front of you, and it's also the one that everyone sees. And don't take the retro-chopper thing to extremes. If you're building an old skool Bobber, put some brakes on the front wheel.

Deciding to buy quality brakes is the easy part, choosing exactly which rotor and caliper combination to buy is much more difficult. When you buy brakes to upgrade that Fat Boy, or for the complete bike you're building in the garage, be sure the components you buy provide better stopping, not just more bling.

Like everything else, there are more caliper choices today than ever before. Everything from the four-piston OEM style to ultra trick four and six-piston assemblies from GMA, Performance Machine, JayBrake and ten or twenty others. In addition, each of the catalog companies and after-market suppliers has their own version of (usually) a four-piston caliper in a polished or plated housing designed to match the lines of the modern billet bikes.

If you're looking for something really different in the brakes department, check out the perimeter brakes offered by Arlen Ness. Instead of attaching the rotor at the hub, it attaches at the

The four piston calipers from Harley-Davidson are high quality and very effective. You can even buy them in chrome plate for extra bling.

edge of the rim. In this way, brake force is transferred to the tire directly, without having to work through the spokes. And the caliper has tremendous leverage because of the large diameter of the rotor.

ROTOR-PAD MATERIAL

The aftermarket offers rotors made from stainless steel, cast iron and even ductile iron. Stainless steel might seem to be the ideal material for brake rotors until you consider the fact that cast or ductile iron makes a better friction material.

Cast iron and ductile iron both offer the brake pad a softer, slightly rougher surface to grab on to. Both materials are very durable. Brake engineers like Bill Gardner from GMA like the ductile iron because of its extreme toughness and the material's ability to radiate the heat of multiple hard stops to the surrounding air. The proverbial trade-off is the tendency of either cast or ductile iron to rust, though this is less a problem now that many companies offer iron rotors with a flash-coat of chrome-nickel.

You need to have a good match between the rotor and pad material. Non-competition pads break down into two groups: organic materials and metallic or sintered-iron materials. The Kevlar pads you often see advertised are considered an organic material, something softer that works well with iron rotors. Sintered iron can be used on stainless rotors, simply because the stainless is so tough.

Unresolved questions about a good match between rotor and pad material (many pads are offered in more than one material) can be answered by a tech at the other end of the 800 number or a good counter person at your favorite chopper shop.

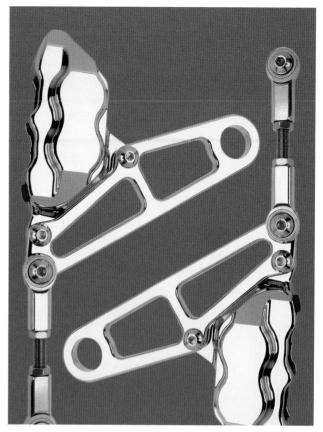

Hawg Halters also provides a wide array of braking hardware for your Harley-Davidson including these billet mounting brackets. Biker's Choice

When Von Dutch built their Cruel World chopper, they installed an enormous 12.6 inch Brembo floating rotor and matching four-piston caliper for the best in contemporary braking. Von Dutch Kustom Motorcycles

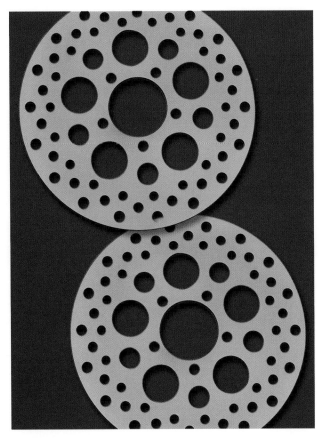

Drilled stainless steel rotors from Biker's Choice are an inexpensive method of improving the looks and braking performance of your custom. Biker's Choice

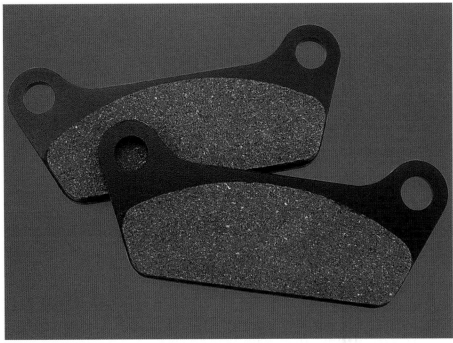

Regardless of which style and brand of brakes you choose to install, using high quality pads in the calipers will ensure safe and confident stopping. Keep the pads matched to the rotors for best performance. Biker's Choice

Despite the iron offerings, many of the shiny rotors seen in the catalogs and on the best custom bikes are made from polished stainless. Though it might not have the idea coefficient of friction, stainless is tough, durable, shiny and doesn't rust.

The caliper and rotor combination that works best for your situation will depend on those unique factors that make it your bike: the weight, how you intend to use the bike, the style of the machine and finally, your budget.

MATCH MAKING

When buying calipers and master cylinders you need to match the size of the master cylinder bore to the caliper(s). Essentially, a smaller diameter master cylinder piston creates more hydraulic pressure but displaces less fluid, than a larger diameter piston (all other things being equal). But before getting too deep into hydraulic ratios it might be helpful to discuss the laws that govern hydraulics. Specifically, you need to keep in mind two facts:

1) Pressure in the brake system is equal over all surfaces of the system.

2) A fluid cannot be compressed to a smaller volume.

Before delving further into hydraulic ratios, let's take a quick look at the fluid itself.

THE FLUID

Brake fluid is a very specialized hydraulic fluid, designed to operate in a very dirty environment and withstand very high temperatures without boiling. When a liquid boils it becomes a gas, a compressible material, sensed by the rider as a very soft or spongy brake lever or pedal. Quality brake fluid will remain viscous at nearly any temperature and resist boiling up to 400 degrees Fahrenheit.

There are three grades of brake fluid commonly available: DOT 3, DOT 4 and DOT 5. DOT 3 and 4 are glycol-based fluids with dry boiling points of 401 and 446 degrees Fahrenheit respectively. Though DOT 3 and 4 fluids are often used in automobiles, you might not want to use them in your motorcycle for two reasons: they are hydroscopic, meaning they absorb water from the environment, and they attack most paints.

When compared to the DOT 3 and 4 brake fluids, DOT 5 brake fluid shows some distinct advantages. DOT 5 fluids are silicone based, which equates to a higher boiling point (500 degrees Fahrenheit, dry), no tendency to absorb water and no reaction when spilled on a painted surface. It costs more and is reputed to be slightly compressible, though street riders never seem to notice any difference in "feel" after switching to silicone fluid.

New Harley-Davidsons have used silicone-based fluid since the early 1980s and the fluid you will find on the shelf of the dealership, or quality aftermarket shop, is probably DOT 5, silicone-based fluid. No matter which fluid you decide to use, stick with that fluid. You should never mix the two types of fluid, and you can't simply drain the system of one type and fill it with the other.

The brake fluid is not compressible which means the pressure at the master cylinder outlet is applied fully to the pistons in the calipers. None of that pressure is "used up" compressing the fluid between the master cylinder and the calipers. This also means that the pressure at the master cylinder outlet is the same pressure that is applied to all the surfaces in the brake system.

When you buy a master cylinder and calipers for the front of that new soft-tail style machine, you not only

There is really only one type of brake fluid to use in your custom bike, DOT 5, silicone-based fluid.

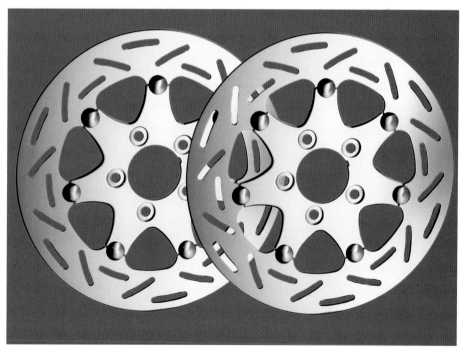

Featuring 7 spokes on its mounting plate, Evil 7 shows us another model of an Arlen Ness brake rotor. Arlen Ness Motorcycles

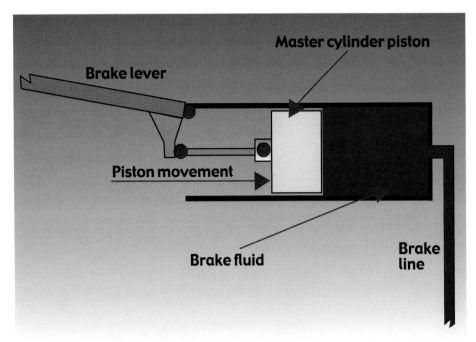

The bigger the master cylinder piston the more fluid is displaced. As the piston size grows however the amount of pressure (all other things being equal) goes down. Output is also affected by the lever ratio, which is why some masters have adjustable pivots.

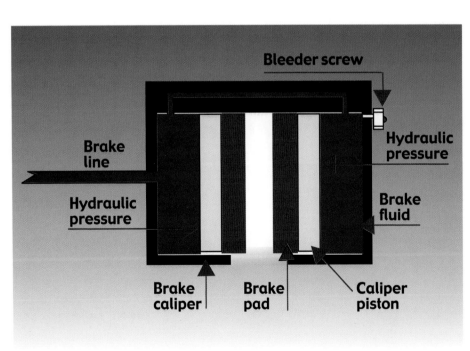

The force created in the master cylinder is transferred fully to the caliper pistons. The more piston area the more net force is created by a certain pressure. The trade off: more pistons (or calipers) require more volume to move all those pistons. That's why the diameter of the master cylinder piston is so important.

need to buy the components that best match your intended use and budget, you also need to buy components that are correctly matched to each other.

HYDRAULIC RATIOS

A demonstration of hydraulic ratios might help explain the importance of correctly matching the master cylinder and the caliper(s). The pressure of the hydraulic fluid at the master cylinder outlet is determined by that old formula from physics class: Pressure = Force/Area. So if you put ten pounds of force on a master cylinder piston with one square inch of area, you have created a pressure of 10psi. If you change the master cylinder to a design with only 1/2 square inch of piston area, then you've created twice the pressure.

Assuming 10psi of pressure in the lines and a caliper with one square inch of piston area, the force on the brake pad will be 10 pounds (Force = Pressure X Area). If you double the piston area you also double the force on the brake pad. Thus the way to achieve maximum force on the brake pads is with a small master cylinder piston working multiple caliper pistons with relatively high total area. For everything you gain, however, you likewise give something up. Small master cylinder pistons don't displace much liquid, and may not provide enough lever travel to fully extend the caliper pistons.

In the real world brake manufacturers and salespeo-

Q&A, Brian from RC Comp.

Brian, start by telling us a just a little bit about yourself and your responsibilities at RC?

I've been at RC for roughly four years, currently I am responsible for the Tech Service and the R&D department. Before that I worked at Holley Automotive for ten years. I held several positions during that time, everything from motorsports manager to engineering associate, the position I held when I left.

Brian, most of the newest calipers are either four or six pistons, tell us the differences from the buyer's perspective?

With six pistons you have more pad area, more friction and better clamping. In terms of braking power, a larger diameter rotor is actually more important than a six-piston caliper. The ultimate brake would be a six-piston caliper and a bigger rotor.

What material do you use for the rotors?

We use 420 Stainless steel. I like the way the stainless dissipates heat. We have people call all the time and they want chrome rotors. Chrome rotors don't work well. The chrome coating means they

One of the trends in modern brakes is the use of a single, larger diameter, rotor on Baggers, which requires a bracket as shown to reposition the caliper.

don't dissipate heat as well as a non-chrome surface. And the chrome turns blue from the heat. The stainless doesn't do that.

What's new in brakes?

People want a single disc instead of dual rotors. The Bagger that we take to the shows has a 21 inch billet front wheel and a single, 13 inch rotor. The rotor is a solid one-piece design but we are also considering a floating design. And we offer an adapter mount so you can keep the stock factory four-piston caliper with the larger diameter rotor. We are seeing a lot of people with baggers who want wheel and brake upgrades. It's the biggest part of our Harley business.

What do you like to see people use for brake lines?

Braided stainless is the most common, and definitely the best bang for the buck. There are better options, but like anything else it comes with a price.

What kind of mistakes do people make when they install or upgrade the brakes?

They make up their own brake lines and make mistakes installing the ends. If someone isn't experienced, I think they should have a shop make up the lines from scratch. Or else purchase lines with crimped ends on them so you can simply screw on the right fitting for the caliper or master cylinder. The brakes are just too important to take a chance with a leak or an end that might blow off on a hard brake application. Too many times when they call with questions, the first thing they're thinking about is the looks. That's just the wrong way to think about brakes. Function should always be first. People don't understand that as you add pistons or calipers with larger pistons to the front brakes, you will likely have to use a master cylinder with a larger bore, because you'll need more volume.

Finally, and you may not believe this, but there are so many people who don't use the front brake. I hear people say they don't use the front brakes because they're afraid of them. I tell them 'your car relies on the front brakes for at least 60% of the stopping' and the same thing is true of motorcycles, without front brakes you're giving up well over half your braking power.

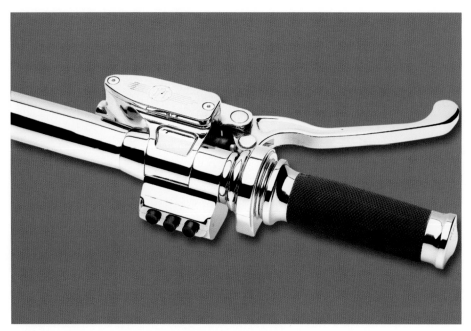

Attractive and also very functional, these contour master cylinders are available with different diameter pistons to better match the caliper(s). Both the master cylinder and the handle bar switches are from PM.

ple skip the computer program and simply rely on certain "rules of thumb" to correctly match the master cylinder with the caliper(s).

Bill Gardner offers the following guidelines: With a single new caliper, 2 or 4 piston design on the rear or front, use a master cylinder with a 5/8 inch bore. If you have dual calipers on the front, whether they're 4 or 6-piston calipers, use a master cylinder with a 3/4 inch piston bore. If in doubt, ask the sales person or manufacturer of your new brake components for a recommendation.

HOSES

Connecting the master cylinder(s) to the caliper(s) are the flexible brake lines. Because the hydraulic pressure in the brake system approaches 1000psi you can only use hoses approved for use in hydraulic brake systems. When buying hydraulic hoses many builders use braided stainless lines from companies like Russell. The braided lines use Teflon inner liners to actually carry the fluid. Unlike the OEM style hoses, which may swell just slightly with brake application, the Teflon liners do not expand at all under hard braking and thus provide a solid, linear feel to the brakes.

Both Russell and Goodridge provide a variety of stainless hose styles. Most common are the universal hoses available in various lengths with a female connector attached at either end. By combining the universal hose

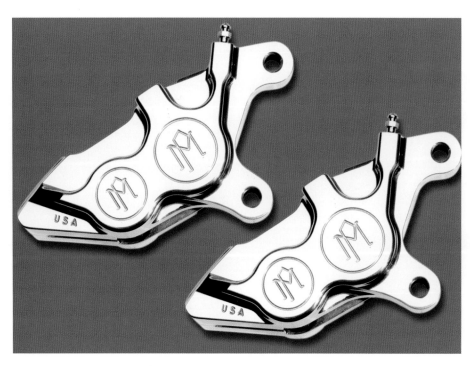

These 4-piston billet calipers use pistons of slightly different diameters to even out the temperature across the brake pad during a hard stop. PM

with the right banjo bolt and connector on either end it's possible to find the right hose/ends combination for nearly any imaginable application.

Even among the universal hoses there are differences. Notably, some hoses are DOT approved, which might be a factor in states with tough inspection laws. Other differences include diameter, hoses come in three sizes known as dash 2, 3 and 4, with 2 being the smallest and 3 the most common by far. If you want pre-made hoses without the additional hardware of a universal hose, some aftermarket shops stock hoses for common lengths and applications, or you can call a company like Performance Machine or Goodridge (some shops also have this capacity) with your specifications and they can make up a hose from scratch.

Goodridge makes a hose with a clear outer cover so the stainless braid won't act like a saw if it rubs against the fender. Or you can buy shrink tubing for brake hoses and use it to coat all or part of your new stainless brake lines. The best way to ensure that the new hose won't act like a saw against your custom paint job is to route it correctly and clamp it securely.

The threads and fittings used for brake lines and banjo bolts are not as standardized as the threads used on common bolts and nuts. For this reason be sure you use matching components - a Russell end for a Russell hose. In today's expanding custom

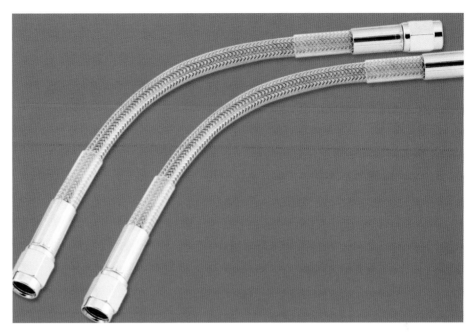

An easy way to enhance the performance of your brake system is by installing braided stainless lines. The braided sleeve protects the inner line. The inner line itself does not expand under pressure like OEM hoses, putting more net pressure to the pads. Biker's Choice

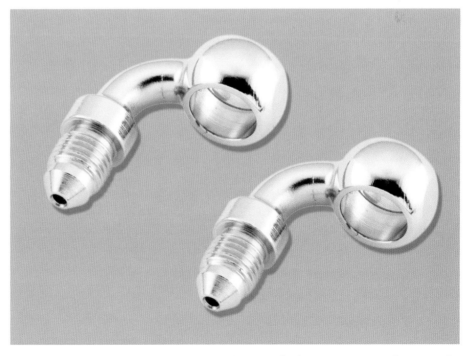

Highly polished banjo fittings are implemented when putting together a modern braking system and provide several benefits for little cost. Biker's Choice

RC components makes these 4-piston calipers, designed to bolt on in place of stock calipers without the need for separate brackets.

The only brake found on Michael Pugliese's Knuckle Sandwich is this small rotor from Performance Machine that is connected to a friction-drive shaft.

motorcycle market, you will even find some machines fitted with solid brake lines versus flexible hose. Not only does this option tidy up the appearance of your scoot, but there is absolutely no expansion when the levers are squeezed hard. Proper tube diameter is crucial in this variation, so be sure to check with those folks who have lots of experience in the use of hard lines before going this route.

Somewhat new on the custom bike scene is the use of "Pro Line," this black plastic line is essentially the inner brake line used on many aftermarket lines, without the braided steel cover. These lines are neat, light and different. Kits can be purchased from Russell and others. The line is easily tucked out of the way for a very neat application. Before making up your own lines though, check out Brian Gaines' comments on line manufacture in his Q&A in this chapter.

FINAL NOTES

When you install those new calipers on the fork or swingarm be sure to center the caliper over the rotor (shims are usually provided for this purpose) and use the correct mounting brackets and bolts. The mounting bolts must be very high quality because the full force of a panic stop is transmitted from the caliper to the chassis through the bracket and bolts. Use bolts that came with the caliper kit or those that are recommended by the manufacturer.

Most aftermarket calipers come in a variety of finishes, including satin, polished and chrome plate. Though it's a small thing, try to match the finish of the caliper to the finish on the wheel and lower legs. If a matching ensemble isn't your goal, try using contrasting finishes for an entirely different look.

Keep all the components matched: the right master cylinder matched to the right calipers to produce the correct pressure and travel at the lever, the right pads matched to the right rotor surface. Keep everything neat and allow no dirt or impurities into the hydraulic part of the system.

In closing it might be instructive to add one more comment from Bill Gardner. "A lot of the questions we get can be traced to poor bleeding procedures. People think the thing has four wheels and they can bleed it just like a car, but bikes use a small master cylinder that doesn't displace much fluid. And some of the bikes have the rear master cylinder and reservoir located lower than the caliper so any air left in the system is trapped there. We recommend that people back bleed the system, forcing fluid in at the bleeder valve with a little tool called an EZ Bleeder. It's quick and easy and it gets the job done right."

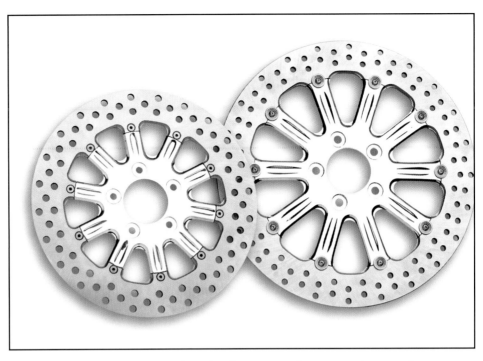

Though other materials are sometimes used, most rotors are made from stainless steel, and many can be purchased in a design that matches the wheels. PM

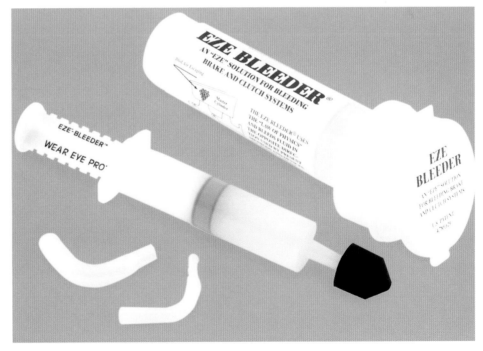

Bleeding brakes is one of those jobs that can be harder than it should be - tools like the Eze Bleeder make the job simpler and more fool proof.

Chapter Six

Wheels & Tires

A Big Part of the Visual Package

Until someone comes around and creates an entirely new way to allow your motorcycle to roll down the highway, it will require a pair of wheels, wrapped with some form of rubber tire. A myriad of options await today's bike builder/rider in both the rim and tire departments. Choosing what works best for you is partially a matter of taste blended with what fits your planned riding style.

California hot rodder and bike builder Bob Bauder said it best: "When you look at a motor-

From RC Components comes a bike designed to demonstrate how a single sided swingarm and single-rotor front brake set up leave the billet wheels fully visible from the right side.

A modified RC Components rim carries Metzeler rubber on both extremes of Chopsmiths' Booby Trap.

less energy into the rest of the motorcycle. A light wheel has the added advantage of being quicker to accelerate when you drop the hammer, which is another reason why drag and road race bikes run the lightest wheels available and even go so far as to use light weight pulleys and sprockets.

CAST OR FORGED?
Aluminum wheels: a.k.a. alloy

Most aluminum wheels are referred to by the name

cycle, a big part of what you see is the wheels." Not only are they a big part of the visual package, they're obviously the only thing holding you up off the highway. So it pays to pay attention before deciding which wheels best dovetail with the rest of that new motorcycle you're building or modifying.

Wheels break down into two broad categories: billet and spoke. Like the rest of the aftermarket, the number of possible choices is large and growing. Style plays a big part here. A forty spoke wheel with a polished or painted rim helps provide a classic appeal to the right bike, while a three-spoke billet aluminum wheel compliments a radical ride with bright orange graphics.

HOW MUCH DO THEY WEIGH?

The weight of the numerous wheel assemblies varies enormously. Why should you care? Assuming you've been paying any attention at all, it's because the weight of your chosen wheels plugs into the ongoing issue of unsprung weight. To repeat what was said in Chapter Four: a lighter wheel/tire/brake assembly will react more quickly to irregularities in the road while feeding

Perhaps in answer to the 300 and 330 tires, many current builders are going the other way, back to slim motorcycles with skinny back tires.

71

Cut from forged billet aluminum, these wheels from RC Components come in all the standard sizes with or without matching rotors and rear pulleys.

"billet" but that doesn't mean that all aluminum wheels are the same in terms of strength, weight and price. What we call billet wheels come in a variety of designs made from more than one alloy and type of aluminum.

What might be called true billet wheels are carved from a billet (or a solid block) of aluminum. In most cases the aluminum in question is 6061 T6. The first four digits identify this as forged aluminum of a certain alloy while the T6 number refers to the heat treating specification.

Billet aluminum wheels are expensive for at least two reasons. First, the blocks of raw, forged aluminum don't come cheap. Second, there's considerable machine time in each wheel, creating the spokes and shapes that define the many models from all the manufacturers.

The cost of an aluminum wheel can be reduced by casting the wheel, generally from an alloy identified as 356 aluminum. This eliminates the expense of buying forged billets of aluminum, though tooling costs can be high. By casting the spokes as part of the wheel design these wheels need less time on the milling machines which further reduces their cost. Most cast wheels have a rim that is an integral part of the assembly instead of being a separate piece

Truly a 3-D design, this Innovator from Xtreme Machine is available in sizes up to 10.5X18 for the rear and 21X3.5 for the front.

bolted or welded to the spokes. Because there may be some porosity in the cast material chrome plating is more difficult. Most aluminum wheels in the aftermarket today are cut from billet rather than cast from 356.

A few years back, most true billet wheels used spokes (or a center section) cut from forged aluminum, bolted or welded to a separate rim assembly. Now, however, there are several methods of manufacturing a true billet wheel with an integral rim (see the interview with Ted Sands from PM for more on the manufacturing processes).

The "split and spin" process starts with a large round disc of billet aluminum mounted into a special lathe or fixture. The fixture spins the raw disc of aluminum while a bit comes in at the edge of the spinning billet and carefully splits the aluminum at the edge. By carefully splitting and rolling this edge, two rim halves are formed at the edge of the spinning aluminum billet. After the rim is formed the incomplete wheel makes its way to a series of CNC operations where the spokes are fashioned in the conventional fashion.

Forging is the other category used to form a billet wheel from one piece of aluminum, but even here, there are two variations on the theme. Pure forging shapes the raw aluminum between a pair of dies. The dies hammer the aluminum and the extremely high pressure gradually molds it into a shape resembling a solid disc with a crude rim at the outer edge. When the dies have created this rough shape, the wheel-to-be is moved to a series of mills and lathes where the entire thing is machined - the rim is finish cut and then the spokes are cut as

they would be for the center section of nearly any billet wheel. Rotary forging rolls the blank into shape with some specialized tooling and a great deal of pressure. Again, once the rough shape is created, the blank is moved through a series of machining operations on CNC equipment.

This "forged" wheel exhibits some very unique qualities. First, the pressure compresses the aluminum and makes it even stronger than it would be in raw condition. Second, because of the density the material can be polished to a high shine and chrome plated with relative ease.

When deciding which wheels to buy consider the fact that it's hard to beat the strength-to-weight ratio of 6061 aluminum, especially after forging. In most cases a true billet wheel is lighter and stronger than a very similar appearing cast wheel. Cast wheels, because of differences in the two alloys, may not be able to match the polished finish seen on a billet wheel. Because 6061 is stronger, billet wheels may offer designs and details that can't be matched in a cast wheel.

When you buy those new aluminum wheels be sure you get what you pay for. If you're paying

If you're looking for a bit of that old-skool hot rod look, try these Legend wheels from RC Components. Sizes range from 16 to 23 inches.

Dave Perewitz put 23 and 20 inch wheels on his Discovery bike and learned a few things along the way: "Rolling Thunder built the frame, and they had to move the swingarm pivot to keep the bike low and still keep the geometry right. You also have to change the gearing because the larger diameter tires raise the gearing quite a bit." Michael S. Keegan

The front wheel measures 23X4 inches. Both wheels, along with the rotors and pulley, are from PM. Michael S. Keegan

billet prices be sure the wheels are billet aluminum. Remember that not all bolt-on wheels actually bolt on. Ask around at some local shops to learn which wheels fit right out of the box especially if you're bolting these to a factory Softail or Bagger.

WHEEL SIZES

Until recently there were a limited number of wheel sizes for V-twin motorcycles. Diameters in the front measured 21, 19 and 16, inches; in back nearly all the wheels and tires measured 16 inches. The growth in the custom wheel market means the "standard" diameters have grown to include 18 inches (sometimes 17) on both the front and the rear. In addition, we have the new really-big wheels and tires to consider. From Avon we have 20 and 23 inch tires for the front and rear, while Metzeler offers their own tall-tires in 21 and 24 inch diameters.

How fat or how tall that rear rubber should be is another decision that must be made early in the planning stage. While fat tires have grown to 300 and bigger, there is a counter-reaction among many builders who strive to build bikes with more reasonable tires in the 180 and 200 range. No matter how wide you want that rear tire to be, be sure the frame is designed to accept the tire, with or without belt drive. Much of this information was covered earlier in the book.

With the exception of the new super tall tires, most front rubber falls into one of four sizes: 16, 18, 19 or 21. Dressers come with 16 inch tires on both ends, as do some of the Softail models. The Custom Softails, whether built in Milwaukee or the local motorcycle shop tend to use a 21 on the front, with the exception of some customs that use 18 inch tires and wheels on both ends. If you want the look of the big 21 inch tire up front but with a little more rubber on the road, Avon manufactures a 120/70X21 that's considerably wider than the typical skinny 90/90X21 we're all grown accustomed to over the years.

Before going to a non-typical tire size like 17 (more commonly seen on sport bikes) or 23, consider that the true diameter of the tire affects the gear ratio and the bike's height. Note Dave Perewitz's comments on page 74. The profile of the tire also needs to match the profile of the fender or the sheet metal just doesn't look right. The 17 inch tires are smaller in diameter than the other, more typical sizes seen on Harley-Davidsons and similar American V-Twins. This means the gearing will be off, unless you compensate when you build the bike. It's also hard to find a fender with an edge-radius that will match the 17 inch tires, though you could use a blank and cut your own radius. Likewise the super-tall tires will have the bike

Unless you like to spend your Sunday mornings polishing aluminum, it's nice to have chrome plated wheels. And if you buy chrome, buy from a quality company with a good warranty as it's sometimes hard to get chrome to stick to aluminum. PM

There are so many great wheels designs available, it makes sense to spend time picking the one that works best with your particular motorcycle. Some are old skool, some are new skool and some are just plain kool. PM

Q&A, Thomas "Ski" Maslowski

Ski, give us a little background on you, how did you come to work at Hoppe & Associates, the Avon Tyre importer.

Well, I worked for two Harley-Davidson dealerships spanning a 15 year period, then I worked for Drag for almost fifteen years. After leaving Drag I managed a sales team here in Minnesota for seven years for Midwest MC Supply out of St. Louis, Mo. and now of course I work for Hoppe & Associates and Avon Tyres. While I was at Drag I tested and sold all the major brands of tires. When I came to Avon I'd already been using Avon Tyres on my own bike. I'd already tested a new tire called the Venom. This was a new premium tire made for use on the heavier Harleys. After testing it would be an understatement to say they performed well in every aspect.

What's the biggest problem people have with tires?

The biggest problem is tire pressure. Not enough. Riders don't check their air pressure often enough. Buy at least a $15.00 gauge and check the pressure every day. It takes only seconds to do and can save a lot of money in the long run.

What is the right pressure?

That's not an easy question to answer. Because of the way our Avons are constructed and the materials we use, they are termed a premium tire. The OEM tire is what comes on the bike from the manufacturer, they are good tires but the manufacturing side of a company needs to keep the cost down as much as possible. When you put Avons on your bike you have stepped up several notches, you are now using one of the better tires in the industry. With an Avon tire, because it is a premium tire, you get better performance, better mileage – and they require higher air pressures.

Typical pressure for our tires would be 42 to 44 in the rear if you're riding solo. For two up riding or a loaded down bike, you need 46 to 50 pounds. In the front we recommend 38-40 solo riding, 40-43 for two up or heavy loads.

Too often people who buy premium tires run them at OEM pressures. If they run ours at 30 to 35 pounds the tires are 10 pounds low from the git-go! Riders who have a question can talk to the service manager at their dealership or directly with the tire importer. Here at Avon we have a tech line they can call

with any questions they may have, from tire pressure to construction or warranty problems.

What makes a premium tire?

First, the construction. Avon uses Aramid, which is a brand name for Kevlar, everyone else has pretty much gone back to using steel or nylon in their tire construction. The actual carcass construction is extremely important, especially the sidewall. With a stronger sidewall the bike doesn't want to "fall off" in the corners.

Second is the rubber. We give the buyer lots of rubber and the compound is an improved version over an OEM type tire. We've also improved our silica-injection process so the tire warms up quicker. Here in the Midwest we ride in the rain a lot. Avon has what we term EAF or an enhanced aqua flow pattern. Remember, the front wheel removes 75 to 80 percent of the water you ride through, with the rear wheel running on basically a wet road with virtually no water film. This way the handling is at it's best.

Can you run a low profile tire on a Bagger?

Yes, FBI (Fat Baggers Incorporated) is running a 200/50ZR17 low profile tire without any issues. You can run low profile tires on a bagger with no problem if the bike has been customized to accept these larger, low profile tires.

How do I pick tires that match, front and rear? And can I run a radial with a non-radial?

In the Avon line all our tire models come with a matching front and rear tire. Whether it's sport touring or the heavier full touring motorcycles, Avon has a matching set. And you can still mix and match, even from one brand to another. People sometimes ask us if you can run a front tire in the rear or vise versa? Our answer to that is yes you can, but if you do you have to run the directional arrow the opposite of what the tire is made for. This is because of the way the tire is constricted and the way the belts overlap. You could get separation at the weld joint if you run

a rear on the front for example with out turning it 180 degrees. This is because that tire was designed to withstand the forces of acceleration but when you put a rear on the front, the biggest force it encounters is braking.

Contrary to what we have been told for years, you can mix a radial with a bias but you must have the radial in the rear and the bias tire on the front, never the other way around. And yes, the radial is a better performing tire. The radial always maintains the largest contact patch on the road.

Where do riders make mistakes with their tires?

Most tire problems come from what I like to call pilot error. Things like riding across long hot stretches of highway with an improperly inflated tire or overloading the motorcycle. What sometimes bothers us as a manufacturer is that riders sometimes want to blame the tire for a problem or warranty issue when in most cases the rider has actually caused or enhanced the problem. A rider in Ohio complained because he didn't get many miles from his new rear tire. When we investigated it further, it turned out he ran the tire at 38 pounds, and he always rode double and pulled a trailer. A really serious and detrimental combination when one wants a lot of mileage out of the tires

Riders will sometimes tell us, 'I don't ride much so I only want a cheap tire.' But remember, if you loose one tire, you only have one left. If cost is that important you can always shop for prices, but try to buy from a local shop. Storage is an issue as well. A tire is just a ring of solidified chemicals. Everything reacts with them. Temperature, UV light, Ozone, or air born chemical molecules react with your tires. Get your bike up on a board and off the concrete somehow during the winter. Avoid the gas fumes and Ozone as much as possible and you will add years to the life of your motorcycle tires.

sitting high up off the pavement, unless, again, you compensate during the design and building part of the project.

In the end the bike's style and frame will dictate the size of the tire. Choosing the wheels and tires is another example of decisions that must be made in concert with all your other choices. When you buy the wheels make sure to tell the dealer or counter person as much as you can about the bike. That way you're likely to get the right wheel with the right hub and hardware the first time. If you're installing a popular rear wheel in a factory frame, ask if the hub is the same dimension as stock, because if it's not you will need new spacers to correctly position the wheel.

Remember that the final width of the tire is affected by the width of the rim it is mounted on. The 200/60X16 Avon is 7.9 inches wide when mounted on a 5.5 inch rim. The widest rim Avon recommends using with that tire is 6.25 inches wide, which will result in the same tire having a width of 8.5 inches. And though a 180X18 and a 200X16 might be roughly the same width, they have a much different profile which affects both the looks of the bike and the way it handles.

WIRE WHEELS -
Spokes, hubs and rims

Not all wheels are billet, and today we have spoke wheels with 40, 80 and 120 spokes (and some limited production wheels with more than 120 spokes), with rims of aluminum or steel. Rim diameters include 16, 17, 18, 19 and 21 inches and widths range from just over two inches to over eight inches across. Spokes come in steel or stainless steel, in round, square and twisted configurations. Though you might have decided on spoke wheels during the planning phase, deciding exactly which spoke wheel to run can be mighty confusing.

Most of the spokes used today are 6/8 gauge, though heavier gauges are available. The best spokes seem to be those with a well-known brand name. At the center of the wheel is the hub, made from either steel or aluminum. Not all hubs are created equal and not all hubs use the same spoke indexing pattern. The Motor Company has used at least three different indexing patterns over the years. In addition, not all spokes will fit all hubs. The hub you use must match the bike, i.e. wide or narrow-style fork and single or double-disc brakes. The hub manufacturer will suggest spokes, some are quite specific as to which spokes must be used with which hubs.

The name that comes up again and again when discussing spokes or wire wheels is Buchanan. Their polished stainless spokes are made in this country, and come in round or twisted-rectangular designs. Again, not all spokes fit all rims or hubs.

Akront, Excel and Sun all make high-quality aluminum rims. Many of the catalog companies offer these rims already laced to

The standard 40 spoke wheel provides a classic look that's hard to beat.

a matching hub with stainless spokes. While the Akront rims come in a polished finish, the Excel aluminum rims come with chrome plate. These already assembled rims come in nearly every available size, including 16X5.5 inches or 18X5.75 inches, both for the rear wheel. Front rims include all the common 16, 18, 19 and 21 inch sizes, with hubs of various widths designed for single or dual rotors. A number of these companies are now offering compete assembled wire wheels with colored rims, either powder coated or anodized, ideal for old-skool bikes.

Chrome plated steel rims come from a variety of manufacturers and are listed in every aftermarket catalog. Sizes of the steel rims tend to stay closer to the most popular stock dimensions, though extra wide steel rims are available from a variety of sources.

Currently quite popular are the 60 and 80 spoke assemblies with chrome plated, or painted, steel rims. Available in various sizes, some of these wire wheels have the distinction of a tubeless designation, made possible by the silicone sealant used to seal the spokes against the rim.

Before buying the newest in 80 or 120 spoke wheel designs remember that all those extra spokes add considerably to both the cost and the weight of a spoke wheel.

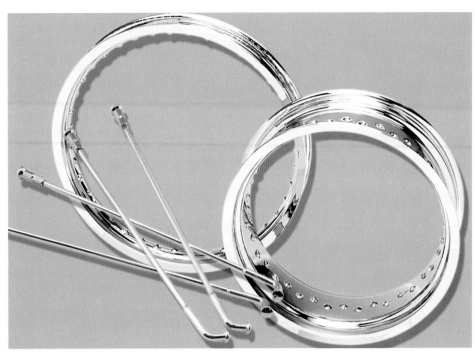

When it comes to assembling wire wheels from scratch, remember that there is more than one spoke size and indexing pattern.

These Styleglide wheels come with 60 spokes for more strength, and rim sizes from 16 to 21 inches, including 18, and widths to 8.5 inches. Spokes come either straight or twisted. Biker's Choice

LACING AND TRUING

While we all like to do as much of our own work as possible, it might pay to farm out at least part of the wheel assembly chores. Specifically, the process of truing a new wheel, assembled from components, is one of those jobs better left to professionals. At the very least, assembling and truing a wheel is a very time-consuming operation for a virgin. If you are having wheels assembled from components, it's possible to lace the wheel with some extra offset to one side, to clear the belt if you're trying to stuff a 200 in place of a 130 on a factory Softail for example.

At the beginning of this section we talked about the major impact the wheels have on the way your bike looks. They also have a major impact on the way it works. The weight of the wheel and tire assemblies affects how the bike accelerates. This same weight, or lack of, affects the way it handles by contributing to unsprung weight.

Though many of the rim and wheel assemblies look the same, they aren't. So take enough time to understand the differences in quality, style and price.

WHEEL BEARINGS AND AXLES

Starting with the 2000 year models, Harley-Davidson started using sealed wheel bearings in place of the old tried and true tapered Timken bear-

At Kokesh MC, outside Minneapolis, they can assemble and true nearly any spoked wheel. They warn however, that not all spokes fit all wheels, be sure you have the right spoke, wheel, and hub combination. Most spokes come with lube for the threads. The factory service manual is a good guide, even if you've done this before.

You need patience and a logical game plan when truing a wheel. Bug from Kokesh explains that, "wheels can be trued with an offset to one side, which might help you clear the belt when adding a wider tire for example."

Q&A, Ted Sands from PM

Ted, as co-founder of PM, can you tell us a little about how the majority of what we call billet wheels are manufactured?

The majority of wheels are called forged billet wheels, but there are actually two different types of forging, rotary and cold forged. With a rotary forge the wheel blank is rolled into the basic shape. Cold forging uses dies and enormous pressure to shape the blank. We start with a raw ingot of 6061 aluminum, about 14 inches in diameter and hammer it with dies into the basic shape of a wheel. The forge is a three story structure, two stories above ground and one below. We buy the tooling and all the work is done to our specifications. We always leave the center at least one inch thick, that way we get more dimension to our wheels. Cold forging involves less metal stretching than a radial forge and makes the strongest forging of all. There is one more process that is sometimes called split and spin, a few low-end wheels are made this way, but it makes a much weaker wheel.

Tell us about heat treating and machining?

Our wheels are heat treated before the machining. We are known for unique and different designs in our wheels, we are able to do that partly because we make our own tooling, and in some cases we modify existing tooling to get a special look to our wheels. We always try to give depth to the spoke shape. I give a lot of the credit to Roland, he designs the wheels with the new speed dots and contrast cuts that people really like.

Is the plating done in house, and what makes for a good plating job, especially on Aluminum?

Chrome plating is not done in house. We have worked with our plating company for years and years, they do a really good job. The key is to have the Aluminum contamination-free and sealed with the first layer of zinc, then copper and triple nickel. The better the base seal the better the odds that the chrome plating will last the life of the wheel.

All of your wheels are one piece?

Yes, but the hub is attached after the wheel is manufactured.

What's new in wheels?

We are in full production on the contrast cut. The starting point is a finished blank, which is then black anodized. Then we put it on the machine so that when it's done, what you see is the black surface contrasted by the cut.

What do you think about the new tall wheels?

I think it's a good direction, these new wheels are bigger in diameter not width, the aftermarket needs to catch up with development of frames, fenders and forks to fit these new size of tires.

The trend with automobiles is going the same way. In terms of width for motorcycles anything over a 300mm is ridiculous to me. Especially if you want to go around corners.

How light or heavy is a good billet wheel?

We have a large range of wheels. Most of our wheels are lighter than any factory wheel and you can save a lot of un-sprung weight. We also have wheels designed to be very light for sport bikes

What makes PM different from all the other wheel companies out there?

We've been doing this for 36 years. And testing, we test the designs so we know it's a safe wheel. The process includes radial and torsional load tests, and impact tests. We are one of the few wheel companies with an in-house test facility.

The Venom R radial rear tire is available in 250, 300 and 330 widths and diameters up to the new 20 inch designs.

ings. When buying wheels, be sure you understand the difference, and if you end up with tapered bearings, don't forget to pack them before installation. Wheels with tapered bearings also have to be adjusted for end play, a process that's best described in any good service manual. There are also two axle sizes available from both the factory and the aftermarket, 3/4 and 1 inch. Just be sure you know what you're buying and that all the components will work together.

Tires

Before buying tires or deciding which tire and wheel combination to run, consider that a low profile 18 inch tire is about the same overall diameter as a 16 inch tire with a standard, fatter, profile. This means the two tires of different "diameters" can be run with essentially the same gearing and the same fenders. As mentioned earlier, 17 inch tires, however, are smaller in diameter than either a 16 or 18. The new tall tires have similar issues, with regard to fenders, chassis set up and gearing, as mentioned elsewhere in this text.

In the past we always recommended against the use of a radial on one end of the bike and a non-radial on the other. In spite of that warning, there are plenty of bikes out there with 250 or 300 Venom R radial tires from Avon on the back, and a non-radial 19 or 21 inch tire on the front, with no apparent ill effects. For more on mixing and matching tires, see the interview with "Ski" from Hoppe & Associates, the Avon tire distributor.

Motorcycle tires, at least the good ones, are rated according to speed and load capacity. Speed ratings start at S, good for

Like most tire companies, Avon makes matched front and rear tires. Note the comments in the text before you decide to use a front tire on the rear or the other way around.

112 miles per hour; H, good for 130 miles per hour; and V, good for 150 miles per hour. Load ratings come down to only two: B and C. B for most of what we call custom bikes and C for those big Dressers destined to carry lots of baggage.

The information published by the manufacturers for each tire includes the ideal rim width. As mentioned, if you mount a given tire on a rim wider than that recommended, the tire does get wider, though you can only go so far.

The majority of V-twin riders don't do much sustained high speed riding so most of them don't have to worry too much about the speed ratings. If you're an exception to this rule, take note of the designations on your tires. Bagger riders need to pay attention to the load rating, especially those that carry heavy gear. V-rated tires provide a nice feeling of insurance for those of us who enjoy, even occasionally, a little high speed cruising down the super slab. A few tires in the catalogs carry no speed rating and no brand name either. These cheap tires seem to us like a very bad place to try and save a few bucks.

The Cruisemax from Dunlop is just that, a tire designed from the start for cruising and touring. Available in 130 X 16 inch front, and 130 to 150 X 16 inch rear sizes, the Cruisemax is designed to give long life and a nice ride. Biker's Choice

Built by Dunlop but branded as a Harley-Davidson tire, the D402 comes in 16 and 21 inch sizes for the front and various 16 inch sizes for the rear. Biker's Choice

83

Chapter Seven

Wiring

The Harness and Components

BASICS OF DC ELECTRICITY

It is not our intention to offer an engineering-level explanation of DC electronic theory. This chapter is intended to aid the individual who is building or modifying a bike and needs a little help getting the electrons to move from the battery to the headlight, or whatever. With this goal in mind we offer a brief overview of electronic theory and a basic explanation of the electronic components you are most likely to encounter as you build or modify that project bike in the garage.

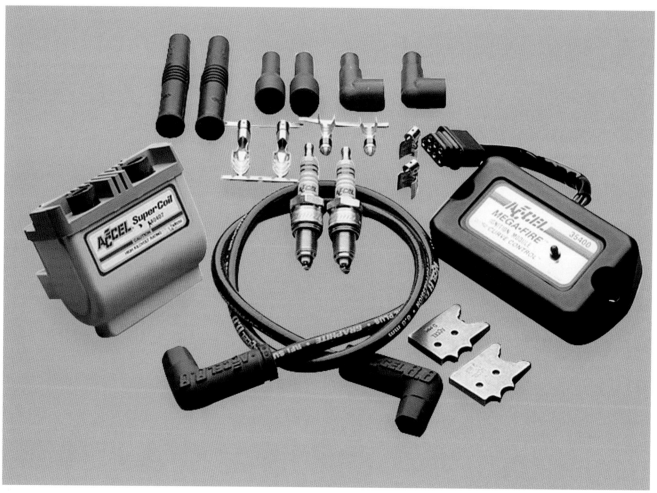

Delivering everything you need in a single package, this ignition set leaves nothing to the imagination. Biker's Choice

WHAT IT IS

To better understand some basics of motorcycle electrical systems and why they are designed the way they are, there are a few basic terms we need to understand first.

Terms.

Voltage (V): the force that pushes electrons through a wire (sometimes called the electromotive force).

Current (I): the volume of electrons moving through the wire, measured in amps.

Resistance (R): the restriction to the flow of electrons measured in ohms.

Most people have heard of the "water through the hose theory." In this analogy the water pressure is the voltage, the volume of water is the current and the kink in the hose is the resistance.

The way these three forces interact is contained in a very simple formula you may remember from Science or Physics class, known as Ohm's law.

Ohm's law: V=IxR or stated another way,
I =V/R and R=V/I

WIRE SIZE CONSIDERATIONS

The size of wire is very important. Basically, the larger the wire, with more strands in the wire, the more current it can carry. Different wire sizes and types are manufactured with different amounts of strands. Most household wire is made of a single heavy strand, good for carrying high voltages and low current. In automotive and motorcycle applications the wire is sized from light to heavy and is always made up of many strands, which is good for carrying higher current flows at relatively low voltage. Multiple strands also makes the wire flexible and less prone to breakage from vibration.

The size of a wire is known as its gauge. Bigger numbers indicate a smaller wire able to carry less current. A 22 gauge wire might be used for a gauge or very small bulb while a 4 or 6 gauge wire would make a good motorcycle battery cable.

Length Current	0-4ft.	4-7ft.	7-10ft.	10-13ft.	13-16ft.	16-19ft.
0-20A	14ga.	12ga.	12ga.	10ga.	10ga.	8ga.
20-35A	12ga.	10ga.	8ga.	8ga.	6ga.	6ga.
35-50A	10ga.	8ga.	8ga.	6ga.	6ga.	4ga.
50-65A	8ga.	8ga.	6ga.	4ga.	4ga.	4ga.
65-85A	6ga.	6ga.	4ga.	4ga.	2ga.	2ga.
85-105A	6ga.	6ga.	4ga.	2ga.	2ga.	2ga.
105-125A	4ga.	4ga.	4ga.	2ga.	2ga.	0ga.
125-150A	2ga.	2ga.	2ga.	2ga.	0ga.	0ga.

Wire size chart from the IASCA handbook. The size of wire used in any circuit is determined by the current load and the length of the wire. This chart is for copper wire (don't use aluminum wire).

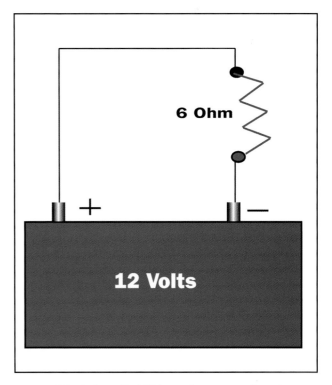

Using Ohm's law (I=V/R) we determine that the current in this impractical circuit is 2 amps.

85

This TXL wire from Painless Performance uses a very high quality, high temperature insulation that is actually thinner than the insulation on the hardware-store wire most of us are familiar with.

Even within a given gauge, different types of wires will have different numbers of strands. Higher quality wire generally contains a larger number of smaller diameter strands. As a general rule of thumb, always use the highest number of strands per wire size as possible.

WIRE SIZE IN A CIRCUIT

The two things that determine the gauge needed for a circuit are the current load the wire will need to carry, and the length of the wire that carries that load (see the wire size chart). More current requires a larger diameter wire (smaller gauge number). The same current, but in a longer piece of wire, will require a larger diameter wire. When in doubt about the diameter of the wire you need for particular application always go larger, not smaller.

The other thing to consider when buying wire is the quality of the insulation. The best automotive grade wire is TXL, with insulation that is thinner, yet more heat (125 degrees C) and abrasion resistant than anything else on the market. A more common rating might be GPT, this is common "auto store" wire with insulation rated at 85 degrees C.

Remember that the new high temperature insulation like that used with TXL is thinner than the insulation used with lesser grades of wire making it hard to determine the gauge of the wire. What looks at first like a 16 gauge wire might actually be 14 gauge wire with the new, thinner insulation.

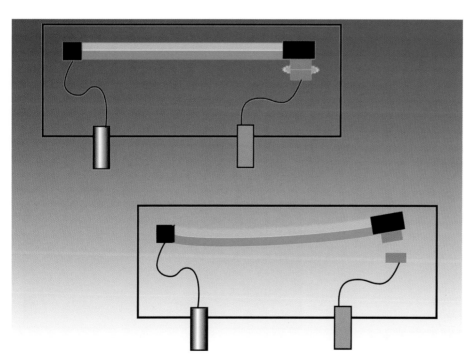

Too much current moving through the bi-metallic strip in this auto-reset circuit breaker creates heat, which causes the dis-similar metals to expand at different rates - and open the circuit.

CIRCUIT PROTECTION DEVICES

Fuses

A fuse is one of the most important parts of any electrical circuit. The fuse is the weak link in the passage of current and is designed to allow only a preset amount of current to flow through the circuit. By using a fuse to regulate current flow, overloads to the circuit are eliminated. A fuse works by having a small conductive strip between the two contacts that is designed to melt at a certain temperature. When current flow reaches a certain maximum level the natural resistance of the strip creates enough heat to melt the strip, thus stopping current flow. If a wire rubs through the insulation and contacts the frame the fuse will blow well before the wire gets hot enough to melt. Without a fuse (or circuit breaker) you run the risk of melting the wires in one or more circuits and possibly starting a fire.

Circuit Breakers

Circuit breakers, like fuses, are designed to protect circuits from overloading. The major difference between fuses and circuit breakers is that fuses are not reusable and circuit breakers are. Circuit breakers have a bimetallic strip that heats up under overload conditions causing a break in the current flow.

Most of the circuit breakers used with V-twins are what you might call automatic reset. This type of circuit breaker will automatically reset itself when the bimetallic strip cools. This is the most commonly used type and will continue to turn current off and on as long as the circuit is overloaded.

Physically smaller circuit breakers are now available in the standard 15 and 30 amp ratings. The smaller size makes it easier to neatly locate these breakers.

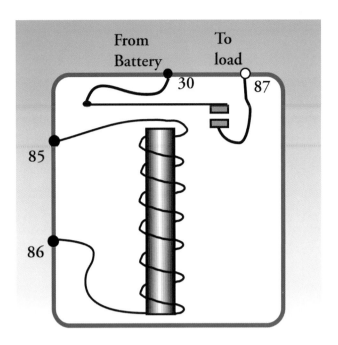

This schematic shows the internal workings of a basic 4-prong electric relay. A small current moving between 85 and 86 (the control side of the relay) creates a magnetic field which closes the load carrying part of the relay.

Circuit breakers come in various sizes, though the capacities are generally either 15 or 30 amps. Most are auto-reset, meaning that as soon as the overload is eliminated the breaker will reset and power will be restored to that circuit.

CIRCUIT CONTROL DEVICES
Relays

A relay can be thought of as a remote switch controlled by another switch. Most relays have two "sides," a control side and a load side. In most cases when you hit the switch you put current through the control side of the relay which then closes the contacts on the load side (check the illustration).

A relay is designed to pass relatively large amounts of current to specific devices, rather than have that current pass through switches and major harnesses. Relays are often used to prevent overloading of circuits or switches. A relay is usually mounted close to the device that requires the high current. Power is transferred directly from the battery source to the device through the relay.

A good example of how a relay is used would be the starter circuit on most V-twins. When you hit the starter button on the bars you're actually sending current from the button to the control side of the starter relay. Current passes through the coil in the control side of the relay to ground creating a magnetic field as it does so. The magnetic field causes the contacts on the load side of the relay to close. With these contacts closed, current moves

from the battery to the starter solenoid (check the diagram). Without the relay the heavy wires needed to power the solenoid would have to run up to the switch in the handle bars. Note: some of the new relays are solid state which eliminates the moving armature and the contacts described above, though they do exactly the same job.

Relays are also a good way to control any circuit with heavy current draw, including accessory lights used on dressers and quartz fog or driving lights. By using a relay to power the lights you need only run the small wires needed for the control side of the relay up to the switch. The current to run the lights moves from the battery or main circuit breaker, through a fuse, through the load side of the relay, and on to the lights.

Solenoids

A solenoid used in a starter circuit is really nothing more than a specialized relay. In the case of a V-twin starter circuit, the solenoid is activated by the relay. Inside the solenoid are two coils of wire (a hold-in and a pull-in winding) with a movable plunger in the center. A copper disc is attached to one end of the solenoid. When the coils are energized, a magnetic field is created which causes the plunger to overcome spring pressure and be drawn into the coils. As this happens the copper disc is brought into contact with two terminals inside the solenoid. One of these terminals is connected to the battery, the other connects to the starter motor. Once the copper disc makes the connection between the battery and the starter, current no longer flows to the pull-in winding and only the hold-in winding is used to hold the disc in place.

In addition to moving the copper disc up against the two larger terminals and thus acting as a switch between the battery and starter, the plunger also

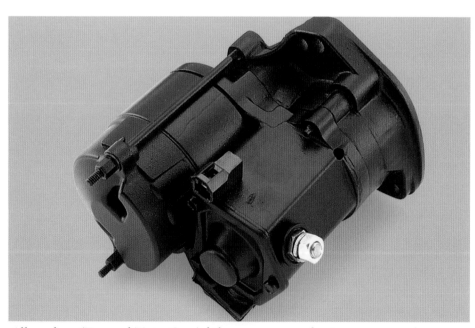

All modern (Evo and Twin Cam) bikes use a gear reduction starter as shown, also available in chrome plate. Heavy duty models of over 2.0 KW are available for that high compression 124, but be sure you have a very high quality battery and heavy enough cables before trying to solve the hard starting problem with a new hi-torque starter.

moves the starter pinion gear into mesh with the gear on the outside of the clutch basket.

Batteries

The heart of any vehicle electrical system is the battery, not just a power source, but also a regulator of voltage in the electrical system.

The battery serves three major functions.

1. The battery is an electricity producing device. The chemical reaction between the lead plates and the electrolyte, a water and sulfuric acid mix, creates electrical current. The voltage is determined by the number of cells.

2. The battery is also a storage device, able to store a large amount of current in its plates and capable of providing this current to the electrical system on demand.

3. In addition the battery is a regulator of current in the system. As the engine rpm or system loads increase or decrease, the voltage and current flow go up and down. The battery acts as a buffer to damp out spikes and stabilize voltage in the system.

Batteries carry a number of ratings. The two most commonly used ratings for motorcycle batteries include cold cranking amps and amp hours. Cold cranking amps is perhaps the most common rating and describes the amount of current the battery can provide for a certain length of time at a given temperature. To determine the rating a battery is chilled to zero degrees Fahrenheit and placed under a load in amps for 30 seconds while maintaining a voltage of 7.2 volts. The larger the rating number the more power that battery can put out to start your thumping big V-twin.

The amp-hour rating describes the number of hours a battery will withstand a certain amperage draw while holding the voltage above a minimum. When the catalogs list the "amp"

Four and five prong relays are available from a variety of sources, and whether they are mechanical or solid state, they all do the same thing and use the same designations on the terminals.

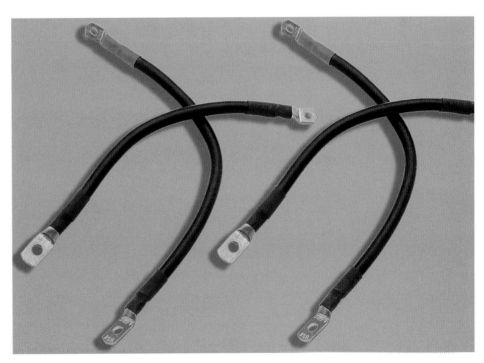

A quality battery is very important when starting a big motor, but remember to use the best cables available in order to minimize voltage drop and heat.

Experienced bike mechanics all say the same thing about hard starting bikes, "buy the best battery you can."

Batteries live a very tough life, asked to deliver awesome amounts of power while living in a heated chamber that vibrates like a paint shaker. Make that life a little easier by setting the battery on a cushion.

rating, they are actually providing the amp-hour ratings provided by the battery manufacturer.

BATTERY BASICS
Construction

Like automotive batteries, motorcycle batteries are constructed of positive and negative plates kept apart by separators, grouped into cells, connected by straps and suspended in a solution of electrolyte. Each cell of the battery produces approximately two volts, by connecting six cells in series a 12 volt battery is created.

Safety warning

Nearly all batteries emit hydrogen gas, explosive to say the least. Gassing is especially likely when the battery is being charged by an external charger but also when the battery is under a load. For these reasons cigarettes, sparks and flames must be kept away from the battery. When jump starting be sure the last connection to be made is the negative cable, connected to the frame or engine of the bike being jumped. That way any spark will happen away from the battery.

Wrenches laid on the battery have the potential to short across the terminals and create an explosion. Also remember that metal jewelry conducts electricity at least as well as a wrench (silver and gold are both excellent conductors), which is one more reason to take off your watch and rings before you start work on the motorcycle. Remember too that batteries contain sulfuric acid, corrosive to metal and damaging to human skin. Spilled acid should be flushed immediately and thoroughly with water.

Battery Chemistry

The plates of the battery are made of lead alloys. These plates are suspended in a solution made up of sulfuric acid and water. When the battery discharges, sulfate (sulfur and oxygen) from the electrolyte combines with the lead on both the positive and negative plates.

As these sulfur compounds are bound to the lead plates oxygen is released from the positive plates. The oxygen mixes with hydrogen in the electrolyte to form water. As this reaction continues the acid becomes weaker and weaker, and more and more sulfate coats the plates. Charging the battery reverses the chemical process, forcing sulfates back into solution with the electrolyte and causing oxygen from the solution to move back onto the positive plate.

The down side to all this charging and discharging business is the inevitable flaking of lead particles from the plates which will diminish the battery's ability to produce and store energy. Further affecting battery performance is the fact that when a battery is left discharged, during the long winter lay up for example, the sulfates penetrate too deeply into the lead plates and cannot be driven back into solution. This is the condition that's often referred to as a "sulfated" battery.

Specific gravity is often used to check the state of charge for non-sealed batteries. Specific gravity simply measures the weight of a liquid as compared to water. The specific gravity of a fully charged battery ranges from 1.260 to 1.280 at 80 degrees Fahrenheit or 1.260 to 1.280 times as heavy as the same volume of water. As the battery becomes discharged the specific gravity drops because the electrolyte has a higher and higher percentage of water. This is also why a discharged battery will freeze on a cold winter's night while a fully charged battery will not.

Low and no-maintenance batteries change the chemical and physical construction of the plates slightly. By adding a chemical like calcium to the plates and changing the structure of the plates themselves, gassing of the battery is greatly reduced. This means a much smaller volume of corrosive/explosive gasses, little or no loss of water, and generally improved performance.

Recombination batteries, sometimes known under the name, valve-regulated, or Gas Recombinant Technology, go even further. These batteries contain all the "electrolyte" in a porous glass mat positioned between the cells. There is no liquid acid in batteries of this type and they can be mounted in nearly any position. Yuasa Battery says these Recombinant batteries can be used in place of non-sealed batteries as long as the bike in question has a good charging circuit and a properly calibrated voltage regulator. In most cases the new sealed batteries do offer better performance than their non-sealed cousins, both in terms of reduced self discharge and increased output for starting.

KEEP IT CHARGED FOR LONG LIFE

All batteries self discharge to some extent. This means a fully charged battery will draw itself down

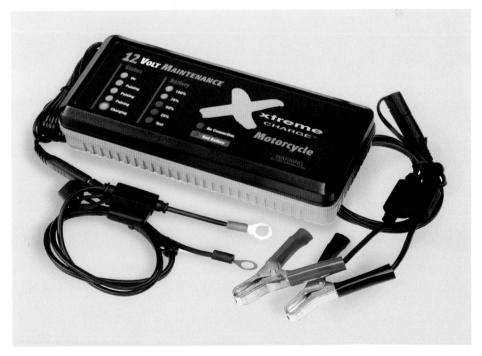

More than just a smart charger that you can leave hooked up to the battery, the Xtreme will evaluate the battery and charge appropriately, using a pulse technology that is said to minimize sulfation on the plates.

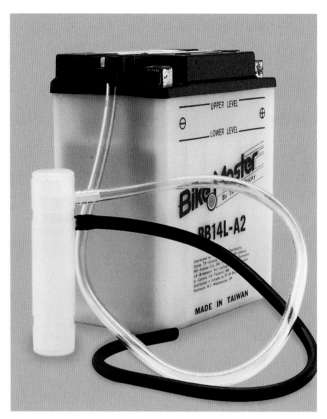

At the heart of every electric start motorcycle is a battery. Yuasa makes models to fit every make and model, and come complete, ready to fill and charge for use. Catch tank collects acid and fumes.

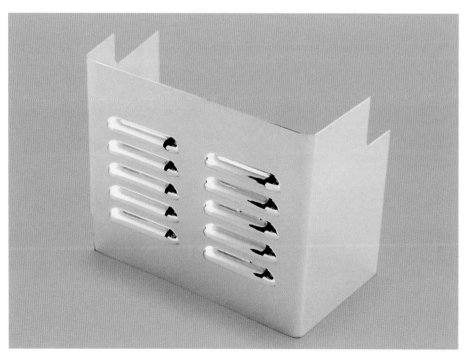

There are all sorts of ways to dress up your rig, don't forget to throw a bit of shine over the otherwise gloomy battery with this louvered cover.
Biker's Choice

to zero voltage over time, even if the battery cables are removed. The answer is to recharge the battery when the bike sits for any extended period. This becomes doubly important with the new fuel injection and radio designs which place a small load (but still a load) on the battery at all times. For long battery life don't allow the battery to run down and don't let it sit for any length of time in a discharged condition.

When your motorcycle sits during those inevitable winter lay ups either make it a point to occasionally charge the battery or connect it to one of the "smart" battery chargers. The cheap chargers, known as ferroresonant designs, do not regulate the charge well enough to avoid damaging your battery when left connected too long. With this style of inexpensive charger, the rate of charge will diminish as the battery comes up to full charge, but the charge rate never tapers off enough to avoid battery melt down. This is true even of the "trickle" chargers. The only chargers you can leave connected without risk of damage to the battery are "battery tender" type chargers.

Other tips for long life are mostly common sense. Keep the battery clean because a film of acid and dirt on the battery case will conduct a small current between the terminals, speeding self discharge. Consider too that temperature increases speed the self-discharge process, so be especially vigilant about charging the battery if the bike sits idle during the warm summer months.

WHICH BATTERY

Batteries for V-twins range in size from the rather small 12N7-4A, designed for kick-start bikes, to the huge HD-12 meant for older Dressers.

Most common among aftermarket and custom bikes is the "16" size battery. Available with different terminal positions and capacity ratings, this is the case size that matches up to the battery box supplied with most aftermarket frames. The 16-B is the standard battery in this group, the less common 16-LA uses the same case with the terminals reversed. Yuasa and others make a variety of batteries in this one case size, each with more or less capacity.

Remember that the expensive high-torque starter can't crank to its full ability unless you provide it with an adequate power source. Even a mild 80 inch V-twin works the starter and battery pretty hard on a warm day. Considering all the money you're spending on this new bike, the cost of the battery is almost insignificant, so buy the best one you can.

Most motorcycle shops and experienced builders will recommend a new battery, before they recommend a big high-torque starter, any time there's a starting problem with a big engine.

MOUNTING THE BATTERY

Battery literature cites the need to mount the battery "away from sources of heat and sparks, and close to the starter." Most motorcycle frames only provide one spot to mount the battery, so the choice of locations is narrowed down to that box under the seat. Just remember that if the battery has a vent tube it should be routed though the frame tubes to the area under the bike

No matter which type of battery you buy put one of the rubber pads, sold in all the catalogs, under the battery to help reduce vibration and extend the life of the battery.

Use the recommended six gauge cables between the battery and solenoid, from the solenoid to the starter, and from the battery to ground. Smaller cable, as mentioned elsewhere, will prevent the battery's full potential from being delivered to the starter. If it's a big motor, consider even heavier cables.

The ground cable must connect to the frame without

the insulating affect of paint between the terminal and the frame itself. Some builders use a star washer between the terminal and the frame to ensure a good ground connection. Speaking of the insulating effect of paint, when the new frame is powder coated or painted be sure to mask off the engine mount(s) where the motor actually sits. This will ensure a good ground connection between the frame and engine. With rubber-mount frames you need to run a separate ground cable from the engine to the frame because of the insulating effects of the rubber mounts. Some shops do this even with non rubber-mount frames.

Remember that if the insulation on the positive cable ever rubs through the frame you have a short lived but very intense arc welder. Use tie-wraps and rubber grommets to ensure that the cables can't be chafed through by sheet metal or the corner of a frame bracket.

STARTERS

Most Evo and Twin Cam engines manufactured in 1994 and later will take the same starter, though you still need to be sure the related components are the right ones (some late Dyna models are the exception up through the 2006 models). The starter

Just because a generator's job is dull doesn't mean the one you install has to be. This model comes wrapped in a chrome shell for a touch of beauty. Biker's Choice

93

you use needs to be matched with the correct inner primary, clutch shell, and compensator sprocket.

The factory Harley-Davidson starter is considered a very good unit by most builders, though the aftermarket offers starters with higher torque ratings for the current crop of mega-motors.

Ask your local shop for a recommendation, preferably a company that's been making starters for more than six months. As pointed out by Don Tima from the Donnie Smith Custom Cycles shop, some aftermarket ignitions (the Crane HI-4 is one) allow the engine to crank for one or two revolutions before the ignition fires which helps almost any V-twin achieve a higher cranking speed.

Some starting trouble can be traced to the small wires people run to the load side of the starter relay. When wiring this side of the relay, from the main circuit breaker to terminal 30, and from terminal 87 to the solenoid, use 12 gauge wire, anything smaller will result in too much voltage drop in the circuit.

One final note, many starters actually started life as metric designs, and as such use a metric thread on the stud. It looks like a plain old 5/16 inch coarse thread – but it's not.

ALTERNATORS

The alternator used to keep the battery charged on your new V-Twin is made up of the same basic components seen in a car or truck alternator, even if the parts from the two applications seem to have little in common.

What is different is the way in which automotive and V-twin systems regulate the voltage and output of the alternator. First, recall that when you cut through a magnetic field with a wire you induce a small current in the wire. Whether you move the wire through the magnetic field or the field over the wire doesn't matter. To increase the output of this simple generator you can either increase the strength of the magnetic field, or you can increase the number or "wires."

Alternators are made up of three components: The stationary stator (the wires), the spinning rotor (the magnetic field), and the regulator.

Most automotive alternators regulate the voltage of the alternator by regulating the current to the rotor. By increasing or decreasing the current to the rotor they control the strength of the magnetic field. V-twin alternators on the other hand use permanent magnets in the rotor, so the strength of the magnetic field is fixed. The voltage is controlled by "shunting" some of the alternator output to ground.

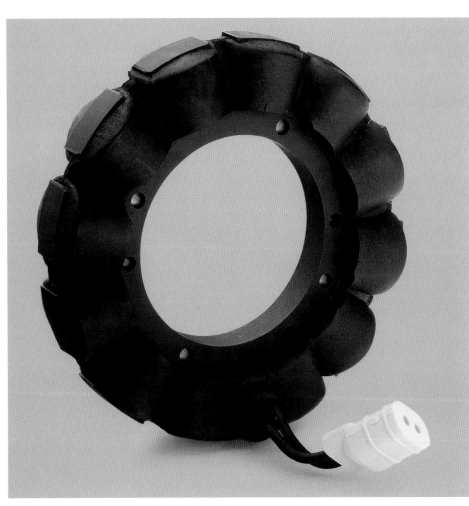

Molded stators from Accel ensure that moisture and debris do little to affect their performance. Plug must match the plug on the regulator. Biker's Choice/Accel

What this means is that the typical V-twin alternator is putting out full power (for that particular RPM) all the time.

The stator, where the electricity is actually generated, is stationary and mounted up against the engine case on the left side. The rotor, the component that spins with the crankshaft, is a large concave disc with permanent magnets which fits over the stator. The third essential component of a V-twin's charging circuit is the regulator, which in this case does more than actually regulate the voltage.

Alternators produce alternating current (AC), which poses a problem as all of our motorcycles run on direct current (DC). Most automotive alternators use two banks of diodes (one-way electrical valves) to convert the AC to DC. V-twin systems use the "regulator" for two jobs: to regulate the voltage output of the system and to rectify the current from AC to DC. Some complete engines, like those from Harley-Davidson, come with the stator and rotor already installed. Most of the engines you buy, however, will require that you buy a complete alternator assembly for the new motor.

WHAT TO BUY

A few words on choosing components. V-twin charging circuits are available in everything from 22 amp models to those with 45 amps and more. For a long time, most factory Softails and most custom bikes ran a 32 amp charging circuit. Today we have new 38 amp systems from both the after-

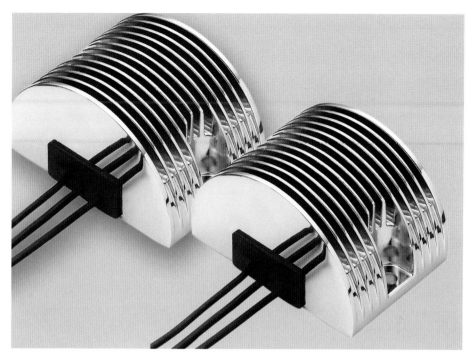

No more little chrome boxes, from Arlen Ness come these contoured regulators with style.

Here you have the basic American V-Twin charging circuit: One rotor with permanent magnets, one stator where the juice is actually produced, and a regulator to control how much juice goes to the battery.

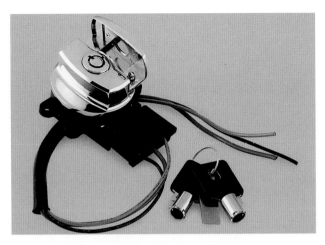

For the builder mixing old and new components, this kit allows the use of a modern switch with an older wiring harness. Biker's Choice

The Thunderheart wiring kit comes with the main module, various harnesses and assorted hardware. Note, not all kits support handlebar switches.

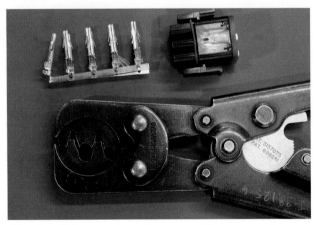

Nearly all harness installations will require crimping connectors to wires, a job best performed in 3 separate steps with a very high quality crimper like that shown here.

market and the factory. The aftermarket systems, some termed "3-phase," put out not just more amperage but more amperage at idle, like a full 25 amps. They get the extra output by redesigning the stator so there are more "wires being cut" by the magnetic field and thus more output. By increasing the output at low rpm these alternators are designed to quickly recharge the battery for bar hoping riders – especially in cases where the bars are very close together.

The regulator must be matched to the stator. Luckily, the molded two-wire connection that connects the regulator with the stator is different depending on the system, designed so you can't plug the wrong regulator into the wrong stator.

Most regulators have three wires, two go to the molded stator connection and one to the main circuit breaker or a positive battery connection. This means that the regulator itself grounds through the base so be sure there's no paint between that base and the frame bracket, some mechanics put a star washer between the regulator and frame. And because the third regulator wire is hot all the time, be sure it can't rub through the frame.

SWITCHES
Choosing the right one

Before buying a switch to serve a particular function, make sure the switch will physically fit in the desired location and that it has enough current carrying capacity for the circuit in question. You also need to make sure the switch will live in a motorcycle environment. That it will stand up to the vibration and weather that motorcycle parts are often subject to. A number of builders put the ignition switch, and possibly the high-low switch, on the coil bracket mounted in the V on the engine's left side. The only problem is that this location can be literally hot, resulting in short ignition switch life.

If you're building a bike from scratch, you have to determine during the mock-up phase where each switch will go. In particular you need to decide if you're going to stay with a basically stock setup where many of the switches are on the bars, or the more "custom" approach of putting the switches on the left side of the engine. This basic decision will affect both the harness you buy and the switches you use.

IGNITION SWITCH

Factory V-twins use a simple on-off ignition switch with an accessory position. These switches are generally designed to be positioned on the bike's left side, or mounted in the dash in the center of the tanks. These on-off switches do not contain a spring-loaded start position and rely on a separate, push-button switch to activate the starter.

Many custom bike builders use an automotive-type switch, available from any auto-parts store, with a built-in start position. The downside to this alternative is the fact that most of these switches are physically larger and may not fit in the intended location. If you elect to take this route be sure the switch you buy is high enough quality to endure the vibration and possible heat of a motorcycle application. By using an automotive ignition switch you can eliminate the starter relay used on stock V-twins. Many mechanics I spoke with, however, prefer to retain the relay to ensure the start side of the switch isn't overloaded by the current draw of the starter solenoid.

Modern motorcycles typically use a hard-wired headlight, meaning the headlight is turned on whenever the ignition is on. The only real switch in the circuit then is the high-low switch. Whether you use a factory-style switch located on the bars or a simple (single throw, double pull) "toggle" switch mounted on the coil bracket, the function is the same. Power comes into the switch and goes out to either the high or low beam of the headlight. Aftermarket switches are available in some catalogs or a Radio Shack store.

THE WIRING HARNESS

A number of new wiring harnesses are available from the aftermarket. Everything from OEM duplicates to abbreviated harnesses that leave a lot of work for the installer to do. You need a harness that's right for your application and comfort level, a harness that doesn't force you to do any more soldering, crimping and adapting than necessary. Always buy a harness that uses the factory color codes to make trouble shooting easier later.

Before deciding which harness to buy, and whether or not to make up a harness in the garage, consider that a poorly built harness can be the kiss of death. Every splice and connection is a potential

Start by striping the insulation off the end of the wire, then position the terminal onto the bare wire and crimp onto the wire.

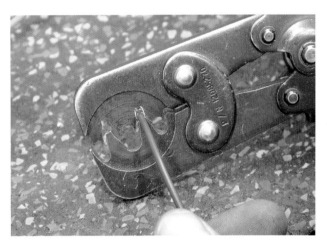

The final step is to crimp the two inner-most tangs of the terminal onto the insulation.

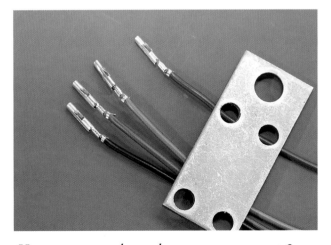

Here you can see the results, a very strong, neat 2-stage crimp. These terminals will slide easily into a terminal block.

site of future failure. Nothing will compromise the reliability of a good motorcycle faster than a cheap or Mickey-Mouse wiring job. Factory harnesses have evolved over the years, though the biggest change came in 1996 when most of the harnesses switched to waterproof Deutsch connectors. Though these might be superior connectors they also make for a more expensive harness.

As we said, the location of the ignition switch is a major factor that must be considered when buying or building a harness. Many universal harnesses found in the catalogs are designed to work with an ignition switch located either on the left side near the seat or in the dash. An OEM harness on the other hand is designed for one specific location. Whether or not you need a complete harness depends to some extent on how "complete" the motorcycle will be. In particular, a stripped bike won't need handle bar switches, or a harness for each side of the bars, while a bike with switches on the bars will. You also have to figure out whether or not the bike will have a speedo and warning lights.

With a factory-style harness there will be some additional handwork for the builder to do. The sub-harnesses for each side of the bars, for example, must be trimmed to the correct length before a small pin is crimped onto the end of each wire in the harness. Each of those pins must then be inserted into the correct position in a plastic terminal block before that block can be snapped into the corresponding block that's part of the main wiring harness or module. And each harness needs to be routed up through the bars.

Anyone who takes this path will need a good wiring diagram to determine where each wire goes in the terminal blocks and other details. This isn't rocket science, but it is tedious work that some first-time builders turn over to an experienced mechanic.

For anyone working on a genuine Harley, the factory manuals contain detailed wiring diagrams. Also, Wolfgang has a new Wiring book coming out, one that covers both customs and bikes from Milwaukee.

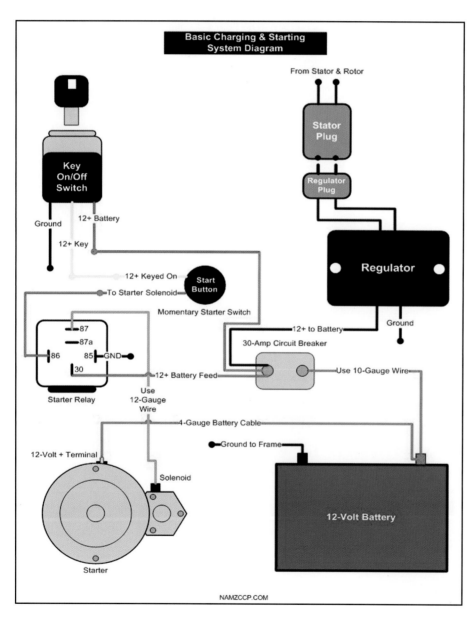

This is the basic starter and charging circuit for nearly all Harleys and V-twins. Unless noted otherwise, all wires are 16 gauge.
Thanks to Jeff Zielinski at NAMZ for both wiring diagrams.

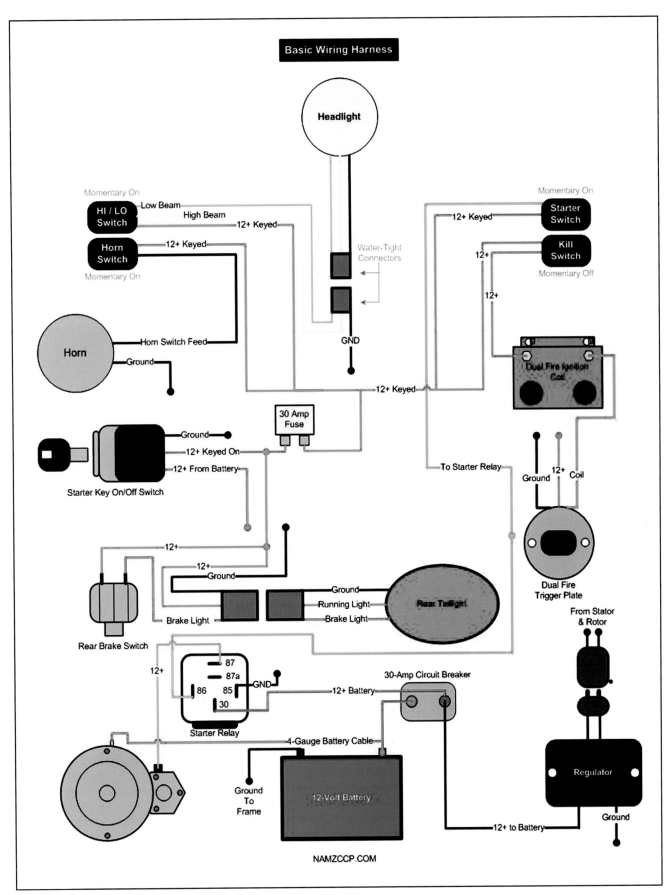

Shown is a good, no-blinkers, wiring schematic. Again, all wires are 16 gauge unless noted otherwise.

Chapter Eight

Sheet Metal

The Right Body Parts for your Chassis

This chapter is about finding and mounting the right sheet metal. "Right" in this case means sheet metal that matches your frame and style of bike, or simply what trips your trigger. Unlike the laws of gravity and electricity, there are very few parameters in this field, and a builder can go as

crazy as he or she wants to. Evidence of this fact can be seen in some of today's wildest customs, or in the "Hamburger" bike that was wrapped with a giant set of bodywork that mimicked the best that char broiling has to offer.

Up until just a few years ago the only sheet

It's hard to have a custom bike without some trick sheet metal. If you're not ready to build a tank by hand, don't panic, there are plenty of designs in the catalogs. Or, by using an aftermarket tank as the starting point, you can add tails or a skirt to build a tank of your own without the hassle of a scratch-built tank.

metal you could buy was the standard replacement parts and a few custom front and rear fenders from Drag Specialties or Arlen Ness.

Today we have unique tin offerings from RWD (Russ Wernimont Design), Kustom Werks, D&D and all the major catalog companies. Everything from sleek bikini fenders to full length Street Sweepers, as well as paneled designs from Milwaukee Iron.

Harley-Davidson makes available all the standard sheet metal seen on their bikes including some fenders without any trim holes. Among the more popular fender designs from Harley-Davidson for bikes with a 16 inch front wheel is the Fat Boy front fender with the flip at the trailing edge and the clean Road Glide fender with no holes.

Gas tanks too have grown into a whole range of new shapes, many of them unimaginable just a few years ago, at a bewildering speed. Fat Bob tanks and faux Fat Bobs are used on a variety of retro bikes. These tanks come in a variety of sizes up to 6 gallons. If you want 'em longer, tails are available from all the standard sources, or you can buy most of the tanks with the tails already installed. One-piece tanks are also available in a variety of shapes. Some are built specifically for a particular application, like late model soft-tail style frames, while others are aimed at the custom market. Most of the catalogs offer steel tanks in short and stretched versions. Arlen Ness, D&D, RWD and others offer very swoopy, long tanks in genuine steel.

Not too many years ago people were scrounging the junk yards in search of Japanese gas tanks that could act as "donor" to a V-twin tank needing a flush-mount gas cap. Today it's much simpler. If you want a flush mount gas cap just be sure the

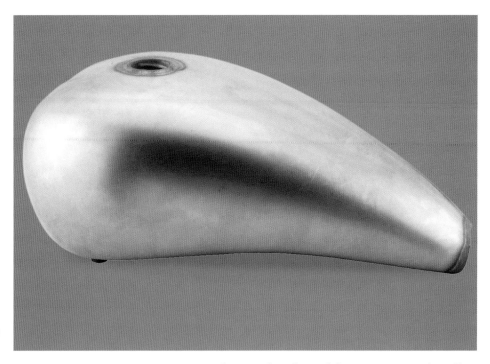

To compliment their line of frames, Daytec also offers a variety of sheet metal that bolts right onto their chassis. Biker's Choice/Daytec

Jesse James, maker of many hand built machines also sells a line of pre-formed fenders allowing the at-home builder to incorporate some attitude into his build. Biker's Choice/Jesse James

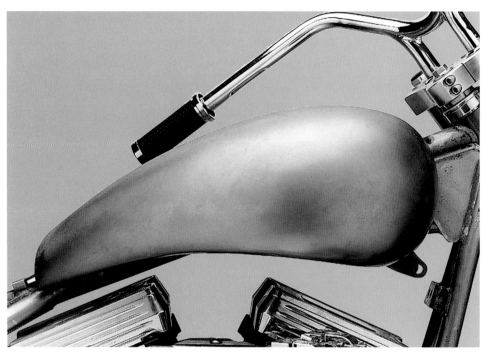

This one-piece tank from Russ Wernimont (RWD) will drop onto the top tube of a late model Softail, or can be used on the custom of your choice. Russ also offers a variety of tank mounting kits, (not shown) available through his web site or through the Drag catalog.

tank you buy comes with, or accepts, one. If you've already got the tank, flush mount gas cap kits are now available (both weld-in and bolt-in) from any of the big catalog distributors.

Building a tank from scratch is a tall order, even if the sides are essentially flat like the old coffin tanks. If you really want a custom tank, buy a good aftermarket tank small enough that you can add on tails or skirts to make it your own. Unless you (or the welder who is helping you) burns through, there are no hassles with leakage and the mounts are already in place as well.

MOUNTING/MOCK-UP

The fenders and gas tank(s) will have to bolt up to the bike, but they should look right too. To repeat the point made earlier in the book, when you're building a scratch-built bike or doing a complete make-over of an existing bike, you have to do a complete mock-up with the bike on a hoist before sending everything out for paint. Many of these parts you buy are custom applications, which means they don't have mounting bosses and even if they do they can't be expected to fit every possible frame. Even the OEM replacement parts may not fit perfectly due to manufacturing tolerances in either the sheet metal or the frame it's bolted to. You don't want

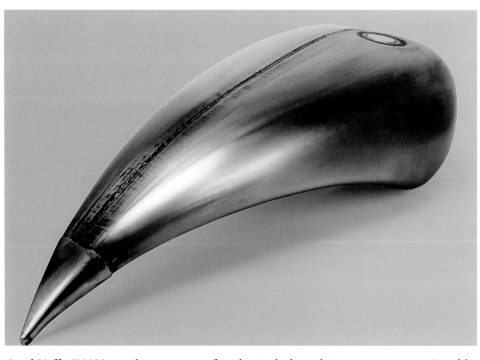

Paul Yaffe (PYO) markets a range of tanks, including this very curvaceous Double Trouble model fabricated from mild steel.

Tank Transformation

Rob Roehl from Donnie Smith Custom Cycles starts this project with a Wernimont tank and a paper pattern.

The nearly finished tail section. Note how the front edge of the tail meets the tank at a curve. And how the tail seems a natural extension of the tank.

Once he has a paper pattern he likes for either side, Rob transfers the outline to 16 ga. cold rolled steel, and begins shaping the steel as shown over a dolly.

The welding is done with a TIG, though gas welding could be used as well. Note how the tacks are spaced evenly, patience is important to avoid warpage.

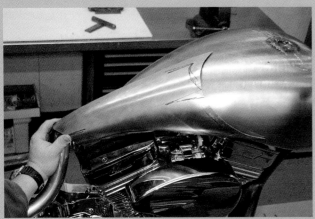

Here's the first rough draft of the new tank tail.

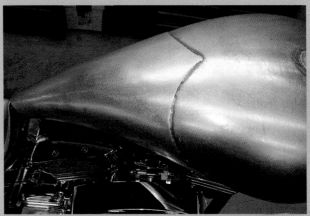

The finished project, minus only a little filler. A relatively easy way to change the tank's shape, without scratch building and with no worries about leakage.

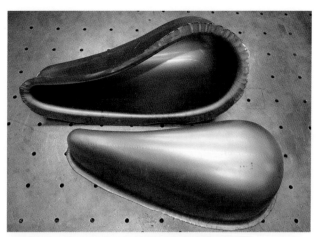

Many of the tanks available from Russ Wernimont or D&D are available as tank halves, so you can alter the width and shape and then weld them together.

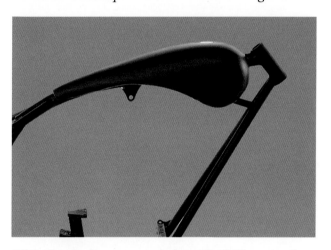

This slim high octane tank from Cyril Huze can be ordered as part of the matching frame, or as a stand alone tank.

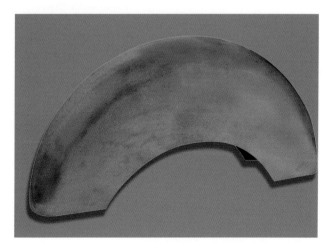

Fender blanks like this allow you to trim them to the shape of your own liking. Some are stamped from heavy steel and need no struts. Kustom Werks

to be drilling mounting holes in the fender after paying big bucks for the pearl paint job.

The mock-up phase also gives you a chance to really examine the bike before you commit to painting all the parts. This exercise works better if you can stand back far enough to really "see" the bike as it will look out on the street. If the rear fender doesn't look right try another one. Spend time mounting each part in slightly different positions. Sometimes a small change in the location of a tank or fender can have a profound effect on the bike's overall appearance. If the bike is going to look good, and look "right," all these parts need to work together in a visual sense and fit the overall look you're trying to achieve.

MOUNTING

Motorcycles, and V-twins in particular, have this nasty habit of vibrating, which makes it crucial that all the parts be mounted correctly. There's nothing worse than a fuel tank that cracks at one of the mounts, or a fender that rubs on the tire.

You have to be sure the tank is well supported. The tank you buy will likely have mounting points already installed, be sure the mounts you weld to the frame are sturdy enough to support the weight of a full gas tank.

Fat Bob style tanks come in two varieties. The most popular and most common are the 1984 and later examples known as "flatsided" tanks. These tanks mount to the frame with rubber grommets, as opposed to the earlier Fat Bob tanks that bolt directly to the frame. If you're mounting a pair of Fat Bob tanks on a bike that came without mounts, kits are available from all the major catalog companies to adapt either early or late-style Fat Bob tanks to any frame.

If mounting the tank to the frame means welding new tabs to the tube, be sure the welding is done by a qualified person. It sounds simple but not just anyone can create a non-brittle weld that won't break later. The same holds for any welding done to the tank itself. The sheet metal is thin and may be under tension and can warp easily if too much heat is applied.

When mounting the fender, remember what was said earlier, tires grow in diameter with speed.

Q&A, Rob Roehl

Rob Roehl is the man responsible for all the sheet metal work to come out of the Donnie Smith shop just north of Minneapolis. From a trimmed fender "blank" to a hand formed gas tank, the shapes, the welding and the mounting are Rob's.

So for a guy buying sheet metal for a custom bike, is sheet metal all the same?

No, quality-wise, you get what you pay for. D&D and Wernimont are more expensive but the parts are US made and they're higher quality. The materials and techniques they use are of a higher quality than what they use in Asia or Mexico. The welding process is nicer with less slag, less clean up and better fitment. With some of the mass-produced stuff, the manufacturing is not real refined, you have to put some work into them to make them fit and make everything right.

Why is the material and the way the parts are built so important to a bike builder?

If you're going to do extensive modifications, like adding an inlay or a flush-mount cap, it's easier if the steel is of higher quality and isn't under a great deal of tension. If the tank is under a lot of tension, it will want to move if you cut it with the plasma cutter or when you start to weld.

When I cut into a European tank the metal is really stiff and hard to work on. The same thing is true of fenders. We use a number of Wernimont, fenders and they tend to be straighter. They also tend to be more workable. Some fenders are stamped from pretty thin steel, which creates a lot of tension in the metal. When you cut them, the metal wants to move right away.

What kind of advice do you have for someone buying sheet metal for a bike-building project?

Buy quality stuff. You don't build a house on a shitty foundation. Don't buy swap meet stuff, you don't know what it's made from, if the steel is dirty the welds will be dirty and the tank won't seal because the welds are porous.

How about some final words of wisdom?

You need lots of practice. Practice your welding. Always work with good parts and materials so you aren't wasting time. Material choices are important, they make all the difference in the world.

Don't use a hard grinder or the big fiberglass sanding discs, those are not meant for sheet metal, they take off too much metal and create a lot of heat. I like to use a soft sander, like a DA with a soft pad. If your metal-working skills are good you don't need to take off all that metal anyway.

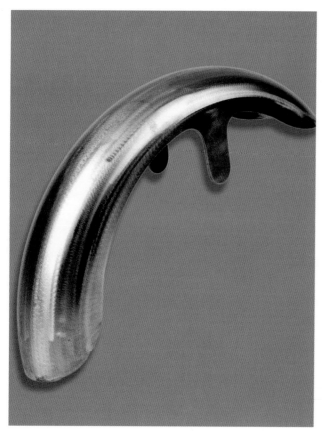

This skinny little fender is called a "thicky" and comes from PYO.

It might look cool to mount the front fender right down there on top of the tire. The trouble comes when you're running down the highway and the tire starts to rub the fender, and the heat blisters the new paint. Or worse, the tire tears the fender off its mounts and stops turning.

When possible, mount the fender (primarily the rear) with button head bolts that point up or out, that way if the tire does touch the bolt it isn't hitting a sharp edge that will tear the tire. You need to know how the geometry of the suspension works – to ensure that the tire can't hit a bolt head or trailing edge of the fender at the end of its travel. And remember that when you hit a big bump the suspension may well move past the standard stop point. These are the kinds of small but important things that people miss all the time.

Speaking of obvious, it's a good idea to use self-locking nuts or plenty of Loctite when installing the fenders. Self-locking Nylock-type nuts are especially handy when mounting plastic or fiberglass fenders because they provide a positive lock without the need to super-tighten the nut. Keep the wires that run inside most rear fenders out of the way by running the wires through small diameter tubing welded up into the corner of the fender. Some aftermarket fenders come with the tubing already in place. If there isn't any tubing located up in the corner of the fender some shops put the wires inside a split plastic housing (intended for automotive applications) and then glue the harness into the corner of the fender with silicone, fiberglass or a product like JB Weld. Factory fenders use little tabs on the inside to hold the wiring harness - be sure the new fat tire won't hit these little tabs.

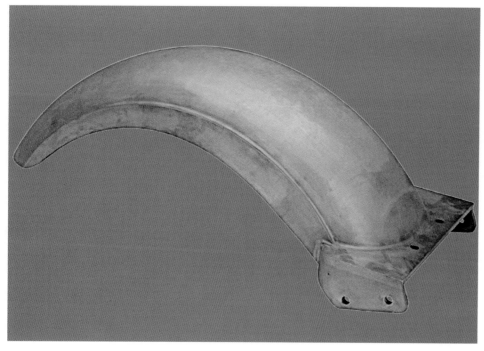

Suitable for a number of soft-tail applications, this fender incorporates the strut into the design. Kustom Werks

METAL FENDERS

There are a number of new companies supplying metal (mostly steel) fenders to the aftermarket that are stamped or rolled. Some of these come from "off shore" and some are domestic, but the quality of most is very good. If you need a recommendation, as to the best quality, ask at a customizing or fabrication shop. To quote Rob Roehl from Donnie Smith's shop, " some of the fenders are really good and some aren't. Some use poor quality steel and some are under tension so if you cut them or try to weld them they warp pretty bad." See Rob's Q&A nearby for more reasons to buy good quality sheet metal.

Sheet metal does more than just keep off the rain or provide a vessel to hold gasoline. The sheet metal and the paint that covers it determine to a large extent what people see when they look at your new bike. Before you buy, take the time to do a sketch of the bike. Some builders take a photo of the rolling chassis, and enlarge that, and then sketch on a piece of tracing paper laid over the enlarged chassis photo. That way the parts will fit the dimensions and proportions of the chassis.

Remember to think as you do the mounting. Gas tanks need to be supported correctly so they don't crack later. Fenders must be installed so the mounting bolts can't ever touch the tire, even when you go over the rail road tracks with the bike loaded down for a camping trip.

If you don't do anything else, spend time with the bike in the mock-up stage. Though the temptation might be to rush the parts to the painter, this is one of those situations where going slow will get the job done sooner, not later.

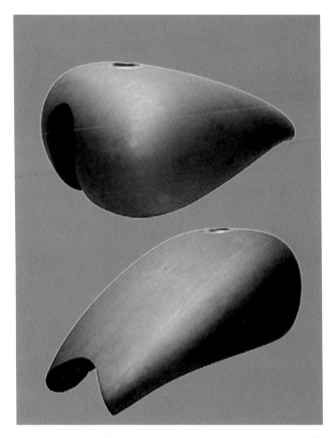

Longer stretched tanks help to stretch out the lines of the bike. Luckily, you can now buy the tanks already stretched in various dimensions. Kustom Werks

When searching for the right fender or sheet metal shape, try cutting the new silhouette from light cardboard. In this case, it's an excellent way to test drive a new gas tank. Small magnets or tape can be used to hold them in place.

Chapter Nine

Frame Fabrication

In the Shop at Fabrication Plus

What follows is a frame fabrication sequence shot at Fabrication Plus, home to the Arlen Ness Y2K frame. The idea here is not to make you a frame fabricator, or a welder, but rather to illustrate the amount of work that goes into a quality frame. Quality takes time and costs money, but often save both in the long run. Maybe we can convince you to spend a little extra when you buy that bare frame, and save yourself a bunch of work in the process.

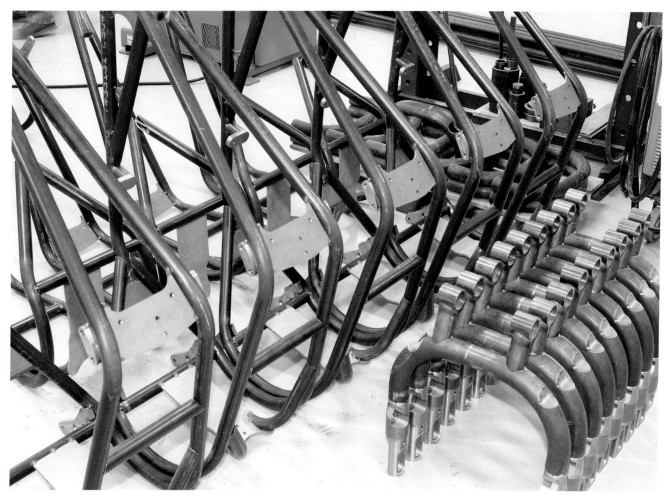

Though manufactured to different dimensions and styles, all the Fabrication Plus frames are manufactured to the same high standards.
Text and photos by Timothy Remus

BUILD A FRAME

If you ask Dave Parks from Fabrication Plus, what goes into a quality frame, he says it's craftsmanship and money. "You can by a frame from China that's only six hundred dollars but the quality is crap. When we deliver our frames to Arlen Ness, they will send them out for powder coating right away and then start in on the assembly. Everything fits and they know that. With a cheap frame, you just about have to be a fabricator by the time you modify the frame so all the parts fit."

At Fab Plus they try to do it right, and doing it right means quality materials and the right procedures applied to a good design.

In this case the quality material is 1020 DOM mild steel tubing. The DOM means drawn over mandrel. As Dave explains, "after they've formed the tubing from flat stock, they run it over a mandrel so it's really round both internally and externally. The operation smoothes out the weld so there's no ridge either on the inside or outside. The material fits into the fixtures precisely because the dimensions are consistent. We always try to buy tubing in quantity, and make sure it's all from the same manufac-

All the parts, and all the fixtures, are drawn up first on the CAD system, then cut on CNC equipment.

The "cope" or recess is cut to a high degree of precision with this Bridgeport equipped with a milling cutter.

109

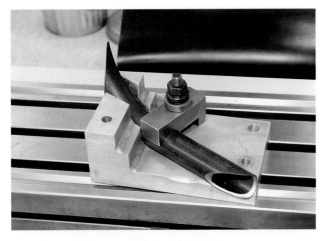

Here's the finished support tube after the cutting operation. The holding fixture is also designed and cut in-house.

...done on a bender that's set up to stop in the same place every time so each bend is exactly the same.

Frame fabrication starts as the tubing is cut to length.

A checking mechanism is used to double check the dimension of the first few components of a long run.

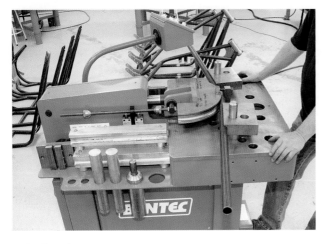

The bending is next...

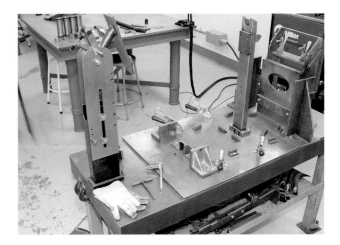

Here's the fixture itself, based on a very flat, very heavy, steel plate.

turing batch. That way each piece has the same spring-back, for example when we're bending so each bend is exactly the same."

EQUIPMENT

Using the proper procedures also means using the right equipment. Dave is especially proud that each machined piece, whether it's part of the frame or part of the fixture that holds the frame, is drawn up first on their own CAD system and cut on their own CNC machines. "This gives us repeatability," says Dave. "Every thing is the same from one day to the next. Our fixtures are so precise that they actually function as another checking station. If a piece of tubing doesn't fit correctly or drop right into the fixture, then something's wrong."

THE WELDING

The actual manufacture of an Arlen Ness frame is done in stages. The two loops that make up most of these frames are bent up and welded into a subassembly, which is set aside. Later the subassembly is put back into the frame jig so all the missing parts can be added.

The welding is done in stages as well. While the parts are in the jig, only tack welding is performed. The final welding is done with the

continue page 114

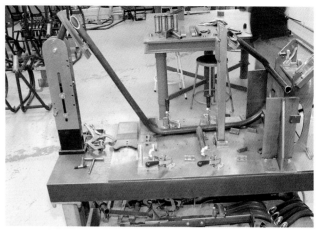

The loops that make up these frames are set into the fixture one at a time.

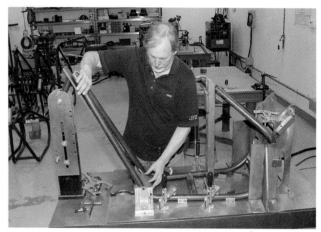

Both loops are clamped securely to the fixture.

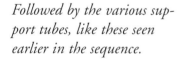

Followed by the various support tubes, like these seen earlier in the sequence.

The components that make up the frame are clamped tightly in place, then this subassembly...

Gradually the collection of tubes takes on the look of a motorcycle frame.

...can be tack welded together and set aside.

Next, the top tube is set in place.

Once it's back in the jig, Robert begins to add necessary parts, like the neck, top tubes and all the rest.

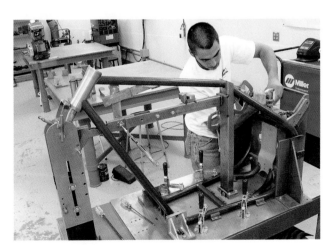

Components are added, then clamped in place.

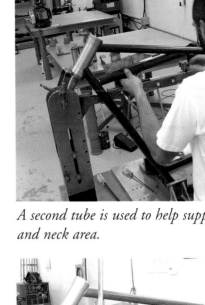

A second tube is used to help support the top tube and neck area.

Magnets are often used to hold a tube until it can be clamped into the fixture.

Here's the finished frame just before tack welding begins.

All the welding done at Fabrication Plus is done with the TIG welder. TIG welding has the advantage of neater welds and a smaller heat affected zone, which translates into less total heat and minimized warpage.

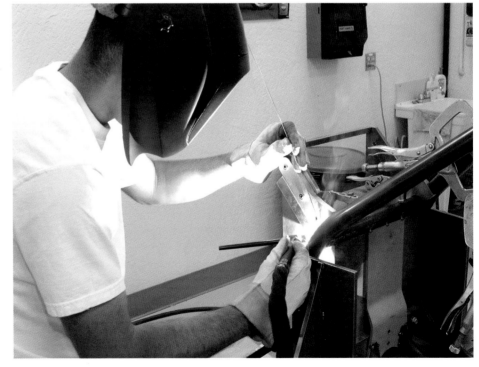

Here, Robert tack welds the neck and support gusset in place.

The finish welding is done with the frame out of the fixture, so it can move in reaction to the heat - otherwise tension can be stored in the frame.

frame sitting on a perfectly flat table. "If we do the final welding in the fixture, the metal can't move as we add heat," explains Dave. "If the metal can't move, we're adding stress to the frame. Because we weld on a flat table, if the welder is adding too much heat in one area, the frame will start to rock on the table. Now the welder knows to move to another part of the frame. We follow a sequence when we weld the frame, and as long as we follow that sequence we get a frame without any added stress and it's straight and true."

SWINGARM MANUFACTURE

Dave likes to keep all the operations in-house, but makes an exception for the swingarms. "The swingarms are made from the same 1020 DOM mild steel as the frame," explains Dave, "but we send them out for the bending. The bending is done with a mandrel. It's like a rattle snake's tail that's pushed up into the tubing before the bending starts so it won't collapse. It's the only way to do those 90 degree, tight-radius bends.

Once all the parts that make up the swingarm are bent and manufactured, everything is clamped onto a fixture, tack welded and finally, finish welded.

The chassis come in various configurations as seen in these partially finished frames.

If you ask Dave what's the hardest part of making a frame, he says it's the initial design and prototyping, "That's just so much work," explains Dave. "It's a whole lot of trial and error, that's where the time investment is. I shudder every time there's a possible change to one of the products we manufacture."

Fabrication Plus is a family affair. Sue Parks, married to Dave, schedules all the work and keeps the books, while their son Robert does most of the CAD work and is one of the best welders in the shop. Together, with a select group of employees, they work to build high quality components they can all be proud of. "One of my non-motorcycle customers wanted me to drop the quality of the parts we build for him," says Dave. "I told him no, we couldn't do it. I mean, how can I tell one of my people that I don't care about how well they do one job, but that they have to do a really good job on another. I can't do it that way."

Though the swingarms are bent up at an outside shop the rest of the work is done at Fab Plus.

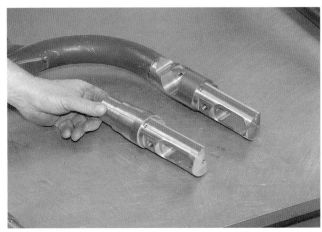

Both the axle housing and the end of the swingarm are machined in-house so the fit is perfect.

Like the frames, once all the components are bent and cut, they are clamped into the fixture as shown for tack welding and later, finish welding.

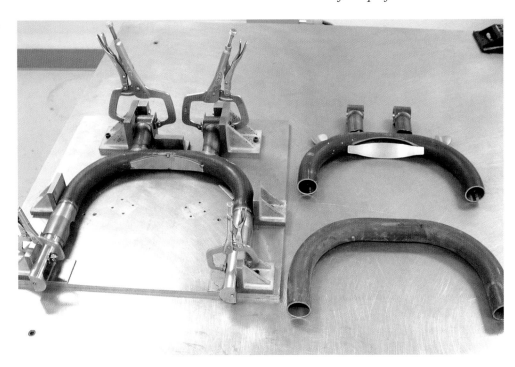

Chapter Ten

Twin Cam Mock-Up Assembly

A Fat-Tire, Hot Rod Bagger

With demand for Baggers at an all time high, Rolling Thunder frame company decided to produce a complete frame kit. This way a shop or individual can easily build a hot rod Bagger without having to buy and cannibalize a factory bike.

The assembly seen here, done at American Thunder in Savage, Minnesota, is not a complete bike assembly, but rather a partial assembly that takes the project from bare frame to a rolling chassis. The Rolling Thunder Bagger frames can be ordered in conservative dimensions and

This is the "finished" picture of the project bike, a 200 tire Bagger built on a Rolling Thunder Bagger frame at the American Thunder shop in Savage, Minnesota.
Text and photos by Timothy Remus

When preparing a frame, one of the first tasks is to drive in the races for the neck bearings.

Before installing the bearings they have to be packed either by hand or with a packer like this one.

A driver like this makes it easy to install the races without any damage.

After packing the lower bearing needs to be driven or pressed onto the stem (these are factory Bagger trees).

assembled to closely resemble a factory Bagger. Or you can order the frame with additional rake, and stretch. This particular frame uses stock dimensions for rake and stretch, but is designed to accept a wider-than-stock 200 rear tire.

PREPARE THE FRAME

The nearby photos document each step of the assembly. Ken Mlsna starts by installing the bearing races in the neck, packing the bearings themselves and then installing the triple trees. The factory manual details a somewhat lengthy procedure to ensure the neck bearings are adjusted so there is no play but also no (or very little) preload. Obviously you don't want slop in the bearings and you don't want any binding as you turn the handle bars. Most experienced mechanics adjust the neck bearings before the tubes go in, and they operate by feel. If you haven't done this before either ask for help or take the time and follow the sequence in the manual.

continued page 123

Next, Ken can install the top bearing and dust cap....

...which can't be completed until the fork is assembled. For now, Ken just gets it snug.

...then he slides the lower tree and bearing up into place and installs the castle nut.

The top tree and nut are installed now...

The factory manual details the procedure for adjusting the nut...

...followed by the "cans" on the lower tree.

After filling the fork tube assemblies Ken slides them up into place, and then tightens the big top nut - with a sealing...

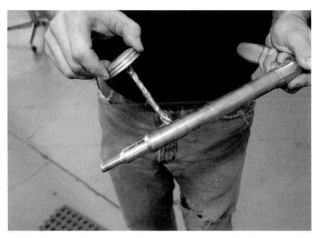

The front axle is coated with anti-seize before installation.

...washer underneath. The pinch bolts in the lower trees are tightened to 35 ft. lbs. after the top nuts are fully tight.

Now the wheel can be lifted up into place, with the correct spacers, the longer spacer goes on the left side, this is a factory wheel and fork.

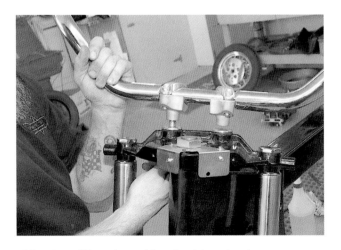

After installing the rubber bushings in the top tree, Ken installed the handle bars as shown.

Next, the axle is slipped through the wheel, the nut is tightened to 50-55 ft. lbs.

After the axle nut is tight, Ken tightens the two 5/16 inch nuts to15-18 ft. lbs. Inside of the hole in the axle should line up with outside of the fork leg.

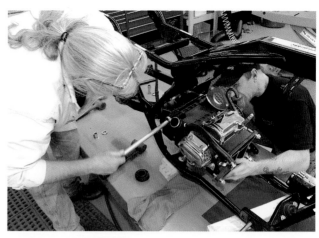

Next the pivot shaft is pushed through. This RT swingarm and shaft assembly is similar to the early factory Evo design.

Swingarm from Rolling Thunder is assembled as shown. The swingarm and the transmission...

Close up shows the shoulder on the pivot shaft and the concave washer, with concave side toward the step on the shaft.

...need to be installed at the same time. An extra set of hands (provided here by Bob Hofmann) helps as well.

The cleveblock must be installed so the notch shown here lines up with the support bracket shown in the next photo.

1. Here's the bracket that supports the cleveblock bushing and ultimately the swingarm and tranny. Note the use of Loctite.

3. Shocks are installed next, be sure the air fitting points forward. Bolts are tightened to 45 ft. lbs. after being treated with Loctite.

2. And here's the brackets installed with bolts tightened to 35 ft. lbs.

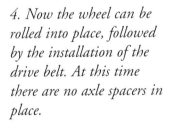

4. Now the wheel can be rolled into place, followed by the installation of the drive belt. At this time there are no axle spacers in place.

1. Progress shot shows the transmission supported by a wood block, and the wheel and belt in place.

2. Ken uses the gauge as shown to ensure the swingarm is straight in the frame. Axle spacers have not been installed.

4. ...then marks the position of the wheel in the frame...

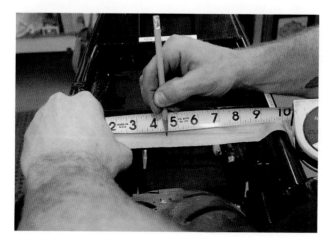

3. Before measuring for spacers, Ken finds the center of the frame...

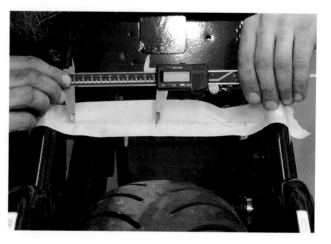

5. ...so he can slide the wheel over and get it in the exact center of the frame.

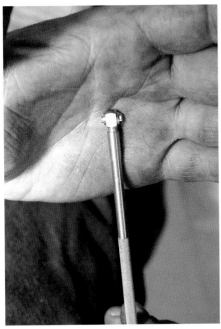

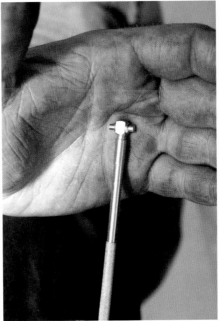

These little snap gauges come in various sizes. Essentially they can be compressed and locked, then released and allowed to extend.

Once extended and locked in place again, just measure the extended gauge with a micrometer and you have the spacer dimension.

Here, Ken used the snap gauge to determine the dimension that the axle spacer needs to be.

THE ASSEMBLY BEGINS

This frame, and this assembly, utilize mostly factory parts. This includes the triple trees, fork tube assemblies, the front wheel and spacers. Once the wheel is set in the fork and the right side fork cap is snug, the axle nut can be tightened, followed by the two 5/16 inch nuts on the fork cap.

Installing the drivetrain in a rubber-mount chassis is considerably different than an Evo softtail type chassis. Instead of bolting the transmission to the frame, you support it with a shaft, the pivot shaft for the swingarm. The whole affair is supported by a pair "cleveblocks" which are contained by heavy caps on either side of the frame. Putting it all together can try a person's patience, so be ready to take a little time, and don't be afraid to ask for help.

Determining the size of the rear wheel spacers is, however, pretty universal. Once the tranny and swingarm are in place Ken makes sure the wheel is straight in the frame, then measures carefully to find the center of the frame and the center of the tire (the tire seam is almost never in the tire's cen-

continued, page 126

Next, he measures the right side, as shown, which requires two spacers, one on either side of the brake caliper carrier.

The spacers are cut from aluminum stock.

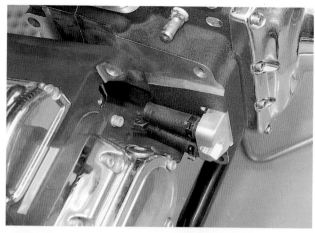

When the engine is slipped into place you have to be sure the two oil lines shown here slide onto the fittings on the tranny.

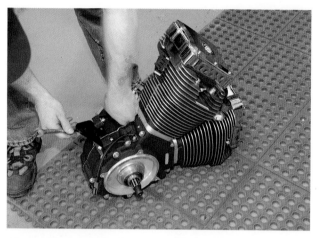

Once the rear wheel is reinstalled and the position double checked, it's time to put the front motor mount bracket on the engine...

Progress shot shows the engine and tranny set loosely in place.

...and set the engine in the frame. A jack under the transmission makes it easy to adjust the transmission position for an easier match.

The alternator stator is next. The two-pin plug is pushed through the case (coated with a little silicone).

Next comes the rotor - the other half of the alternator.

...and the seal.

Inner primary assembly is next. Before installing the mainshaft bearing one of the snap rings is installed.

Don't forget the bushing for the starter and the small seal.

Now the bearing can be installed, followed by the other snap ring...

Because this bike will run a 200 tire, Ken installs a spacer between the engine cases and the inner primary.

Progress shot shows the inner primary ready to go on.

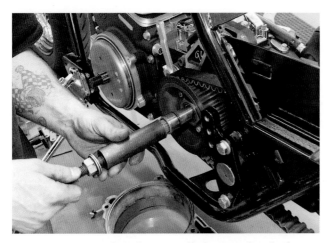

Ken uses a special tool to install the race for the bearing in the inner primary.

ter). Now it's just a matter of sliding the wheel on the axle until it is centered, then measuring for spacers as shown.

MOTOR TIME

The motor installation is next. Not just any old Twin Cam, this particular example is a 124 inch from S&S, guaranteed to make this Bagger haul down the highway like the hottest of soft-tails. Ken and Bob Hofmann explain that it's easier to install the motor "if you install the front mounting plate first, and save installation of the oil filter mount until later."

With the motor in place Ken installs the stator for the alternator, then the rotor and finally the primary drive. The 200 tire used on this bike means a "wide tire kit" needs to be used. The kit includes a set of spacers and a transmission with a longer main shaft (and 5th gear) which effectively moves the drive pulley over to the left, which provides clearance between the belt and the wider tire. All these assorted parts are shown in nearby photos.

If you're working with a bare inner primary, be sure to install the correct bushings, bearings and seals before installation. You also have to remember to use an O-ring on either side of the

continued, page 129

There is a spec in the manual as to the position of the race, or you can use the base of the puller tool (for removing the race) as a checking device to ensure the race is positioned correctly on the shaft.

This is the wide tire kit needed to install the 200 tire. You also need a longer starter connector (shown later).

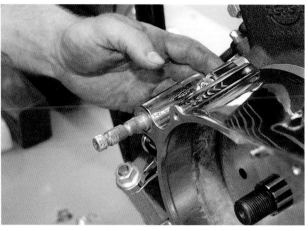

Sometimes we cheat a little for the photos, it's actually easier to install the shift shaft before the inner primary is bolted on.

With the spacers shown in the earlier photo positioned between the inner primary and the engine and tranny, Ken can install...

Now the primary drive assembly can be slipped up and onto the two shafts.

...the inner primary and tighten the bolts.

The big compensator sprocket nut is right hand threads, the clutch hub nut, however, is a lefty.

The tool shown in the inset is a lock, so the clutch hub nut can be torqued to 70 - 80 ft. lbs and the compensator to 165.

...followed by the adjuster assembly. The initial adjustment is to screw the threaded adjuster...

The adjuster shown here is used to move the "shoe" up or down and adjust the primary chain tension.

...in until it just touches the actuator rod and then back off 1/2 turn, then lock it in place as shown.

The clutch actuator shaft slides into the mainshaft...

The starter and jackshaft assembly. The longer connector, needed due to the wide tire kit, is indicated by the arrow.

engine-to-inner-primary spacer. Also, some mechanics use a dab of silicone where the inner primary and spacer meet the engine and transmission.

The inner primary bolts are tightened to 18-21ft. lbs. and locked in place with small lock tabs (the internal ones at least). Installing the primary drive is pretty straightforward, and well illustrated by the nearby photos. The shoe mounted to the inner primary does have a front and a back, and should be installed so the cold primary chain has about 5/8-7/8 inches of up and down play.

Adjusting the clutch is actually a two-step process, the first step is performed as part of the primary drive installation as shown in the nearby photo.

STARTER ASSEMBLY

The starter is a gear reduction design with a multi-piece drive assembly. The starter motor comes in from the right side while the drive comes in from the left before the primary case is buttoned up. The assembly includes two connector sleeves as shown, and each goes in only one way. Ken warns that, "it's easy to snap the long bolt that holds the drive together, which is why I never use more than 70 inch pounds to tighten it."

Both of the connectors should have a snap ring installed as shown...

...the connector on the right is a little longer than stock because of the wide tire kit.

The starter goes in from the right side. The connectors seen in the picture above only go in one way. The smaller one should have the chamfered end on the starter.

Here you can see the jackshaft assembly being installed. The smaller of the two connectors is already on the starter.

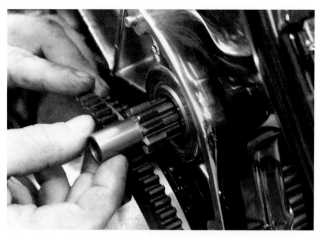

Next the spring and the starter drive are slipped into place.

The snap ring in the large connector is off-center, the shorter side of the connector should be installed toward the starter...

And held in place by the long bolt shown here. Note the tab on the outer washer and the notch in the sealing washer.

...when installed the outer edge of the large diameter connector should be flush with the support as shown.

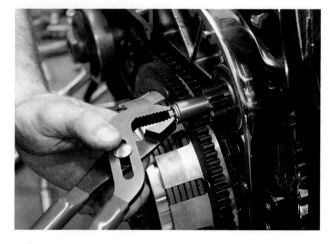

There is another tab on the outermost washer that is bent over to lock the bolt in place. Tighten to 70 in. lbs.

Before buttoning up the primary and installing the outer cover, Ken pulls the starter drive gear out against the spring tension, turns it about 90 degrees and then lets it go. He goes through this process four or five times. Each time the drive should snap back into place. If it doesn't it's likely to hang up in use.

One of the advantages of using a Twin Cam drivetrain is the fact that you don't have to worry about the alignment of the engine and transmission and whether or not the inner primary bolts up square to both units. Because this is a rubber-mount however, there is the issue of engine and transmission alignment within the chassis. Basically there are two adjustable links (which should be replaced if there's any doubt as to their condition) that allow you to move the motor and tranny in two planes. The best how-to guide for this is the factory service manual with its detailed procedure.

The new chassis from Rolling Thunder allows the modern Bagger rider to have his (or her) cake and eat it too. Now you can have a Bagger with all the comforts we take for granted, and the added punch of a big-ass fuel-injected Twin Cam motor. The only thing missing in the recipe is a Tru-Track link to ensure stable high-speed handling.

Outer primary bolts are tightened to 120 in. lbs.

Finished shot shows the right side with the drivetrain fully assembled.

The left side of our Bagger on steroids: 124 cubic inches of plush comfort.

Chapter Eleven

Soft-tail Chassis Mock up

Assembled in the Raw

Anybody can bolt on a fender. Well, almost anybody. Assembling a big-twin powered chassis, however, especially with an Evo and five-speed, is a little more challenging. To show you how it's done by the people who know, we spent a day with Rob Roehl in the Donnie Smith shop.

The idea is to demonstrate how Rob deals with certain alignment issues that crop up whenever you're building this type of bike. This is only a mock up assembly, because you do have to go through this process before all the parts go out for paint.

The finished mock-up assembly. At this point Rob knows the engine and transmission are mounted correctly in the frame, that the primary alignment is correct, that the wheel is in the center of the frame and that the belt tracks true. Text and photos by Timothy Remus

Rob starts with a 250 tire Daytec RSD frame. The motor is a 124 from TP Engineering, mated to a Roadmax transmission. Sometimes when you're doing a mock up assembly, the engine and/or transmission may not have arrived yet. A lot of shops and individuals use any Evo engine and transmission they can find for the mock up, thinking that, what the hell, they're all the same. Rob has other ideas. "I like to use the real engine and transmission whenever possible," explains Rob. "There is some tolerance in those parts, so that two motors don't necessarily fit the frame exactly the same."

Regarding the alignment of the engine and transmission, and the rear wheel, Rob follows a specific sequence. First, he sets the motor in the frame. It should sit flat on all four mounting points. The transmission is next and should likewise sit flat on the mounts. "If they don't sit flat I look to see if there's a little slag or something on the mount," explains Rob. Next the four engine mounting bolts are snugged down.

Now the inner primary can be bolted up to both the engine and transmission, don't forget any spacer needed between the engine and the inside of the inner primary.

With the motor snug and the inner primary tight, Rob now looks to see if there is any gap under the transmission mounting bolts, explaining as he does, "usually the engine mounts are OK, if there are any shims needed it's under the transmission mounts." Finally, he fully tightens the engine mounting bolts and checks again for any light under the transmission mounting points.

Rob doesn't add shims unless the gap measures more then .010 inches (measured with a feeler gauge). And the shims should be hardened shims like those that come with some of the better brake calipers. Finally the transmission can be tightened down and Rob starts on the rear wheel alignment procedure, one that is best explained by the nearby photos.

Remember to save the shims and note their position, so you can get humpty dumpty back together again after paint. Speaking of paint, you will have to mask off the motor mounts before painting, or sand off the paint after painting, so the engine and transmission sit on bare metal, not .025 inches worth of urethane.

This mock-up project starts with a Daytec RSD, 250 tire, Goliath frame.

Rob Roehl from Donnie Smith Custom Cycles, sets the 124 TP engine in the frame. The rest of us will need a friend to help lift the motor into place.

Once the motor is in place Rob can drop the bolts into place. Gardner-Westcott (and others) make bolt kits specifically for engine mounting.

The transmission is a Roadmax, RSD, five-speed.

The inner primary is next...

Rob advises builders to, "use the actual engine and transmission during the mock up if possible, so there is no change in the way things fit later."

...note, there is a 1/2 inch spacer used between the inner primary and the engine. With a 300 tire there is generally no spacer used.

The upper motor mount is next, Rob leaves the bolts loose for now.

The inner primary bolts can be installed now.

At this point Rob knows the engine and tranny are sitting flat on their mounts, and that the engine mounting bolts are snug. The inner primary bolts...

...between the transmission case and the mounting plate. Finally the transmission mounting bolts can be tightened.

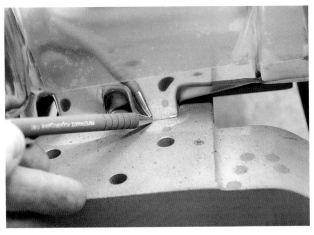

...can be tightened, now he checks to be sure the transmission did not lift up off any mounting points.

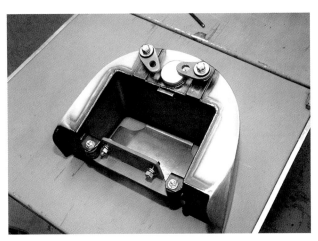

The oil tank came with the Daytec frame kit.

The engine mounting bolts are tightened now, and Rob checks again that the tranny is sitting flat on it's mounts. If there's more than .010 inches of clearance a hardened shim (not part of a beer can) is placed...

Rob recommends putting the oil tank in before the swingarm.

Here you can see the bracket that supports the back of the oil tank. The fame holes are a little too large so there's room to adjust the position of the tank.

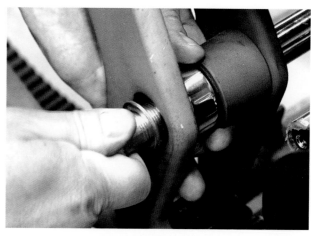

...and then slips the bolt through the pivot bearing, and through the spacer before threading it into the cross-shaft.

The swingarm is supported by two large pivot bolts that thread into the cross-shaft.

The right side spacer is a unique Daytec design. The inner collar is threaded so the spacer can change dimension - no need for multiple shims.

Rob slips the swingarm in place...

For this project we are using a pair of standard-issue soft-tail shocks.

1. Here you can see how the shock bolts mount to the swingarm. With a typical soft-tail suspension the shocks get longer as the wheel moves up.

2. Before putting the wheel in the frame, Rob makes sure the pulley is positioned so there will be at least 1/16th inch of clearance between the belt and the tire.

3. Now the wheel, a new Talon design from Donnie Smith, is rolled into place.

5. Once the belt is adjusted and tracking fairly straight, Rob uses a piece of tubing as shown to indicate the frame's centerline. "The goal is a tire that's in the exact center of the frame (priority one) and a belt that tracks straight."

4. With the axle is in place, and no axle spacers, Rob adjusts the belt tension, gets the wheel straight in the frame and close to being centered.

The alignment sequence continues as Rob marks the exact center of the tire - the seam is almost never in the center...

Next, Rob measures for spacers...

...as shown by this photo.

...because this bike will use a drive-sprocket brake, there is no rear caliper carrier and only one axle spacer on either side of the wheel.

Now it's a matter of sliding the wheel on the axle so it's in the exact center of the frame.

Rob has John Galvin cut spacers on the lathe from one inch aluminum tubing.

Rob has to back-off the axle adjustment, pull the axle...

...to make sure the axle is in the same position from one side to the other. Then it's time to check the way the belt tracks.

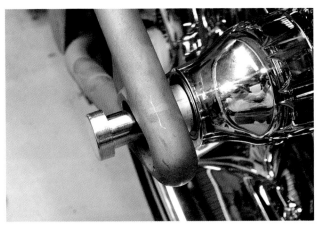

...install the spacers and reinstall the one inch axle.

"With a lot of these RSD bikes the belt will track to one side on the front pulley and to the other side in back. I don't worry as long as the belt isn't rubbing up against the edge of either pulley."

Time now to readjust the axle, using the tool shown...

The strutless rear fender (from D&D) came with the frame kit and is designed to mount to the frame's cross-bar.

The fender comes with separate internal struts, which Rob likely won't use as this is going to be a solo-seat bike.

Time now to stand back and check the fender and it's position on the bike. The importance of these "look-see" sessions can't be over emphasized.

"I use a 2-1/4 inch spacer for one-up bikes that generally leaves enough clearance. But it's essential that you pull the shocks and bottom the suspension...

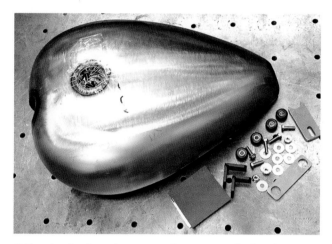

Like the fender, the gas tank came with this frame kit.

... after the fender is installed so you know the tire can't hit the bottom of the fender or any hardware."

The kit also includes some pretty nice tank-mounting hardware.

Bottom of the tank shows the built-in mounting points.

Here's a look at the front mount. the notched steel plate will eventually be welded to the bottom of the top tube.

Daytec provides two pieces of pure silicone padding that is used to keep the tank up off the top tube. Two of these pads were actually used.

Here you can see what the finished mount will look like after welding. Some of the mount that protrudes below the bottom of the tank can be trimmed off.

Here's the first look-see. "This is a nice tank with a good shape. Because it's high quality, it would be a good tank to modify with tails or an extension."

At this point we can see the basic silhouette. We know that the driveline alignment is OK, also that the tank and rear fender fit.

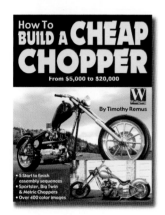

HOW TO BUILD A CHEAP CHOPPER

Choppers don't have to cost $30,000. In fact, a chopper built from the right parts can be assembled for as little as $5,000. *How to Build a Cheap Chopper* documents the construction of 4 inexpensive choppers with complete start-to-finish sequences photographed in the shops of Donnie Smith, Brian Klock and Dave Perewitz.

Least expensive is the metric chopper, based on a Japanese 4-cylinder engine and transmission installed in an hardtail frame. Next up, price wise, are 2 bikes built using Buell/Sportster drivetrains. The recipe here is simple, combine one used Buell, or Sportster, with a hardtail frame for an almost instant chopper. The big twin chopper is the least cheap of the 4, yet it's still far less expensive than most bikes built today.

Twelve Chapters   144 Pages $24.95   Over 400 photos-100% color

ADVANCED CUSTOM M-C ASSEMBLY & FABRICATION MANUAL

What started in the mid-90s when a few people decided to build "stock Softails" from aftermarket parts – because they couldn't buy one at the dealer – has evolved into a full blown industry. Today, every small town has a Chopper or Custom bike shop and every cable TV channel has a Biker-Build-Off series. No longer content to build copies of stock motorcycles, today's builder wants a motorcycle that's longer, lower and sexier than anything approved by a factory design team.

Wolfgang and Tim Remus were there at the very beginning of the trend with their Ultimate V-Twin Motorcycle book. Today they're back with Advanced Custom Motorcycle Assembly & Fabrication. Part catalog, part service manual and part inspiration, this new book offers help with planning the project, getting the right look and actually assembling that custom bike you've dreamed about for years.

Nine Chapters   144 Pages $24.95   Over 400 photos-100% color

HOP-UP & CUSTOMIZE YOUR H-D BAGGER

Baggers don't have to be slow, and they don't have to look like every other Dresser in the parking lot. Take your Bagger from slow to show with a few more cubic inches, a little paint and some well placed accessories. Whether you're looking for additional power or more visual pizzazz, the answers and ideas you need are contained in this new book from Tim Remus.

Follow the project bike from start to finish, including a complete dyno test and remapping of the fuel injections. Includes two 95 inch engine make overs.

How to:
• Pick the best accessories for the best value
• Install a lowering kit
• Do custom paint on a budget
• Create a unique design for your bike

Eight Chapters   144 Pages $24.95   Over 400 full-color photos

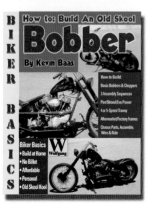

HOW TO BUILD AN OLD SKOOL BOBBER

Old Skool is kool. A fact celebrated by Wolfgang Publications in their new book. No theme bikes here, learn how to build a real American motorcycle based on a Panhead, Shovelhead or Evo engine. Don't buy expensive new parts, build your own bobber or chopper from mix-and-match swap-meet parts.

Written by Kevin Baas, the Kennedy High School shop teacher with the Build-a-Chopper class, this book takes a back-to-basics approach to motorcycle assembly. Follow along as Kevin explains which engines fit which frames, and which transmission and primary drive is the best fit behind a particular V-Twin. The book includes three start-to-finish assembly sequences.

Ten Chapters   144 Pages $24.95   Over 350 color images - 100% color

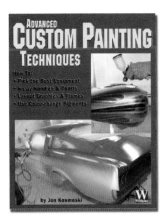

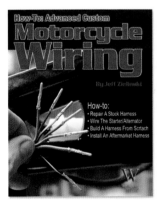
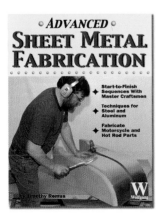

Sources

American Thunder
Custom Motorcycles
1244 Hwy 13 South
Savage, MN 55378
877-389-0138 - 952-746-7786
www.americanthunder.us

American Family Insurance
Michelle
6230 10th St N #430
Oakdale, MN 55128
866-899-3631

Arlen Ness Motorcycle
6050 Dublin Blvd.
Dublin, CA 94568
952-479-6350
www.arlenness.com

Avon Tyres
Thomas "Ski" Maslowski
www.avonmotorcycle.com
smaslowski@avonmotorcycleusa.com
1-800-624-7470 main office

Bob's Shop
2018 South 1st St.
Milwaukee, WI 53207
414-587-3019

Buchanan's Spoke & Rim, Inc.
805 W. Eighth Street
Azusa, California 91702
626-969-4655
www.buchananspokes.com

Chopsmiths
100 Gasoline Alley, Suite B
Indianapolis, IN 46222
317-246-7737
www.handbuiltmotorcycles.com

Cyril Huze Custom, Inc.
Tel: 561.392.5557
Fax: 561.392.9923
www.cyrilhuze.com

Darkside Performance
P.O. Box 11324
Daytona Beach, FL 32120
386-527-5877
www.dpasylum.com

Donnie Smith Custom Cycles Inc.
10594 Radisson Rd. NE
Blaine, MN 55449
763-786-6002
Fax: 763-786-0660
www.donniesmith.com

Extreme Cycle
110 Cross Street
Aurora, IL 60504
630-859-8497
www.extremecycletech.com

Fat Baggers, Inc.
138 E. Lincoln Avenue
Chariton, IA 50049
www.fatbaggers.com
641-774-7499

Great Northern Insurance
Barb
10301 University Av NE
Blaine, MN 55434
763 717 6942

GMA Engineering
13526 A Street
Omaha NE 68144
402-330-5105
www.gmabrakes.com

J&P Cycles
13225 Circle Drive
Anamosa, IA 52205
800-397-4844
www.jpcycles.com

Johnny Legend Customs
26W. 220 Arrow Glen Court
Wheaton, IL 60187
630-217-7627
www.johnnylegend.com

Klock Werks
915 S. Kimball
Mitchell, SD 57301
605-996-3700
www.kustomcycles.com

Kokesh Motorcycle
763-786-9050
www.kokeshmotorcycle.com

Kustomwerks
1200 South Park Dr.
Kernersville, NC 27284
Inquiries: 336-996-8690
www.kustomwerks.com

Motorcycle Works
Mine Creek Business Park
21519 E. 931 Cir.
Pleasanton, Kansas
913-352-6788

NAMZ Custom Cycle Products
169 Boro Line Road, Suite B
King of Prussia, PA 19406
610-265-7100
www.namzcustomcycleproducts.com

Painless Performance
2501 Ludelle St
Fort Worth, Texas 76105
817-244-6212

Paul Yaffe Originals
2211 East Indian School Road
Phoenix, Arizona 85016
602-840-4205
For online orders - x:233
www.paulyaffeoriginals.com

Performance Machine
6892 Marlin Circle
La Palma, CA 90623
714-523-3000
www.performancemachine.com

Precious Metal Customs
488 Hendon Road
Woodstock, GA 30188
678-687-9361
www.preciousmetalcustoms.com

RC Components
373 Mitch McConnell Way
Bowling Green, KY 42101
1-888-721-6495 (toll free)
www.rccomponents.com

Redneck Engineering
107 Nix Rd.
Liberty, SC 29657
864-843-3001
www.redneckenginuity.com

Revolution Manufacturing
e-mail:
Mike@RevolutionSpeed.com
www.revolutionspeed.com

Rolling Thunder Frames
1810 Ford Blvd.
Chateauguay, Quebec
J6J 422 Canada
450-699-7045
www.rollingthunderframes.com

Russ Wernimont
38429 Innovation Court
Murrieta, CA 92563
www.russwernimont.com

S&S Cycle, Inc.
14025 County Hwy. G
Viola, Wisconsin 54664
608-627-2080
www.sscycle.com

Strip Club Choppers
15622 Computer Lane
Huntington Beach, CA 92649
714-908-5534
www.stripclubchoppers.com

Ted Tine Motorsports
244 Middlesex Turnpike
Chester, CT 16412
860-526-2060
www.tedtine.com

TP Engineering
4 Finance Drive
Danbury, CT 06810 USA
203.744.4960
www.tpeng.com

True-Track, Inc.
Wil Phillips
11490 Burbank Bl. Ste 6E
North Hollywood, CA 91601
818-623-0697
www.true-track.com

Von Dutch Kustom Cycles
10743 Edison Court
Rancho Cucamongo, CA 91730
909-481-0600
www.vondutchkustomcycles.com

Xtreme Machine Wheels
2265 W Morton Av
Jacksonville, IL 62650
info@xtrememachineuse.com
xtrememachineusa.com
217-291-0200

XtremeCharge
1100 S. Kimball Ave
Southlake, TX 76092-9009
888-287-9314
www.XCMotorcycle.com